Enjoy the Ride
and the Read

Live Love Laugh

Jean Davidson

Jean Davidson first rode on one of her family's famous motorcycles at age three. She is the granddaughter of Harley-Davidson founder and President Walter Davidson and the daughter of Harley-Davidson Vice President of Manufacturing Gordon McLay Davidson.

Grandfather Walter Davidson and Me, 1938

Growing Up Harley-Davidson

Memoirs of a Motorcycle Dynasty

By Jean Davidson

Foreword by Arthur Harley Davidson

Voyageur Press

Edited by Michael Dregni
Designed by Maria Friedrich
Printed in Hong Kong

02   03   04   05   06   10   9   8   7   6

Library of Congress Cataloging-in-Publication Data

Davidson, Jean, 1937-
     Growing up Harley-Davidson : memoirs of a motorcycle dynasty / by Jean
     Davidson ; foreword by Arthur Davidson.
          p. cm.
     Includes bibliographical references and index.
     ISBN 0-89658-569-7
     1. Davidson, Jean, 1937—Childhood and youth. 2. Harley-Davidson
Incorporated–History. 3. Motorcyclists–United States–Family relation-
ships. 4. Davidson family. 5. Harley family. I. Title.

TL140.D34 A3 2001
629.227'5'092273–dc21
[B]
                                                                    2001017729

Distributed in Canada by Raincoast Books, 9050 Shaughnessy Street, Vancouver, B.C.
V6P 6E5

Published by Voyageur Press, Inc.
123 North Second Street, P.O. Box 338, Stillwater, MN 55082 U.S.A.
651-430-2210, fax 651-430-2211
books@voyageurpress.com
www.voyageurpress.com

Educators, fundraisers, premium and gift buyers, publicists, and marketing managers:
Looking for creative products and new sales ideas? Voyageur Press books are available at special discounts when purchased in quantities, and special editions can be created to your specifications. For details contact the marketing department at 800-888-9653.

Legal Notice
This is not an official publication of Harley-Davidson. The name Harley-Davidson®, as well as certain names, model designations, and logo designs, are the property of H-D Michigan Inc. ("Harley-Davidson"). We use them for identification purposes only. Neither the publisher nor this book are in any way affiliated with Harley-Davidson, Inc., or H-D Michigan Inc.

Dedication

This book is dedicated to everyone who has ever had a dream, for our dreams are the inspirations that make us who we are. Education is something that will help you achieve your goal, but without a dream there is no goal. So this book is dedicated to dreamers who, with motivation, perseverance, and commitment, will make their dream a reality and feel a great sense of fulfillment.

It is also dedicated to the memory of my grandfather Walter Davidson, father Gordon Davidson, mother, and other people who have had such an affect on who I am today.

Frontispiece:
Jean Davidson and 1963 Harley-Davidson FLH Panhead Duo-Glide. Motorcycle courtesy of Competition Cycle. (Photograph by Ken Webb and Norm Zierk)

The Joys of Motorcycling

Acknowledgments

I would like to thank my mother, Doris Davidson, for collecting and saving all the family photos and original papers; my sister, Barbara Davidson Baumann, for all her efforts in organizing and documenting these materials; and all the other relatives and friends of the founders who kept diaries and records sharing their feelings so future generations could feel the excitement of those times. Bessie Davidson, the youngest sister of the founding Davidson brothers, researched a family tree.

I am also deeply grateful to Arthur H. Davidson, who is the only surviving son of the original founders. We spent time together at his Virgin Island home while he shared many stories of the Harley-Davidson founders and their children. His father, Arthur, was the young pattern maker who with his best friend Bill Harley, my grandfather Walter, and another brother William developed the Harley-Davidson Motorcycle.

I would also like to thank Harley-Davidson historians Jerry Hatfield and Herbert Wagner for their assistance in checking technical and historical facts.

My heartfelt thanks to all of you who have been so supportive of my efforts to follow one of my dreams of bringing these stories to life in print for all to enjoy.

Contents

Memoirs of a Motorcycle Dynasty

By Arthur Harley Davidson

Jeanie Davidson and I have collaborated on this wonderfully different book on the now-famous Harley-Davidson motor cycles, the company founders, and their dynasties.

Gordon Davidson, Jeanie's dad, was my first cousin, although he was a few years my senior. From her early years, Jeanie was always a favorite of mine, demonstrating spunk, initiative, inquisitiveness, independence, and an enormous interest in nature all of her life.

Giving credence to the many stories about this group of Scottish Davidsons and their English pal Bill Harley has been my primary assignment since Jeanie and I undertook this project 'lo these many years. We hope that, together, we have prepared a human side of these families that we trust may intrigue Harley-Davidson riders everywhere.

In loving dedication,
Arthur H. Davidson

PS: Yep, the "H" is really for "Harley."

Out For A Ride
A couple zips along a country road on their Harley-Davidson fitted with an early sidecar.

Motorcycles as a Way of Life

My earliest memories are not of birds chirping outside my nursery window or my mother cooing to me in my crib. No, my earliest memories are of the roar of a Harley-Davidson V-twin motorcycle engine as my dad rode to and from work. My dad was Gordon McLay Davidson, and work for him was the Harley-Davidson Motor Company. We are part of the Davidson family; my dad was the eldest son of Harley-Davidson founder Walter Davidson, the firm's first president.

When I was very young, my dad would put me behind him on the seat of his Harley-Davidson and say, "Hang on!" I was too small to see around him so I would just lay my head against his back and feel the vibrations through his leather jacket. Even at such a young age, I loved the sound of that engine and the excitement that I felt on a Harley-Davidson. As far back as I remember, motorcycles have been a way of life for my family. I grew up on a motorcycle, as did my father, my grandfather, and my cousins.

Whenever our families got together through the years, I heard many a tale about my family history and the beginnings of the Harley-Davidson motorcycle. They were exciting stories, and soon I wanted to find out more. This led me on a quest to meet with distant relatives and friends of the founders who were gracious enough to share their memories of my relatives and

Off to Work, 1940

Motorcycles were a way of life for our family. Here, my dad heads off to work on his Harley while my sister Barbara bids him goodbye.

the Harley family in the early years of the Harley-Davidson legacy.

The family story I am about to share goes back generations to Alexander "Sandy" Davidson, a carpenter by trade who came from Brechin, a village in Scotland. At the age of fifty-one, he brought his family to the United States to give his children a better chance to follow their dreams. His children, their children, and their families would work and play together in traditional roles while each one contributed in his or her own unique way to build a product loved the world over.

This American Dream–come-true has affected all the generations of my family. I am proud to be a member of this historic family and am honored to be sharing family stories that have been handed down through the years.

While researching these stories, I was amazed at how my own personal belief comes forward over and over again. That is, each one of us has a unique gift or talent and it is up to us to discover it, develop it, and then share it. By listening to our hearts and following our dreams, great personal satisfaction will come. This will lead to happiness and contentment, and like a radiating glow, will spread outward, touching many people.

Does this sound like the life story of the Harley-Davidson motorcycle, which is now loved all over the world? I think it does. It is the classic American tale—a success story of motivation, perseverance, and commitment to a dream, the American Dream of freedom to choose to be and do whatever you desire in this great land of opportunity.

This is a true story of the promise that if you follow your dreams, those dreams will come true. It is also my story of growing up in a family where the sound of the Harley-Davidson motorcycle was a way of life.

Jean Davidson

The Well-Dressed Motorcyclist, 1916
My grandfather Walter sits astride a 1916 V-twin. (Courtesy of the Harley-Davidson Motor Company Archives; © 2001 Harley-Davidson; all rights reserved)

Davidson Clan Family Tree

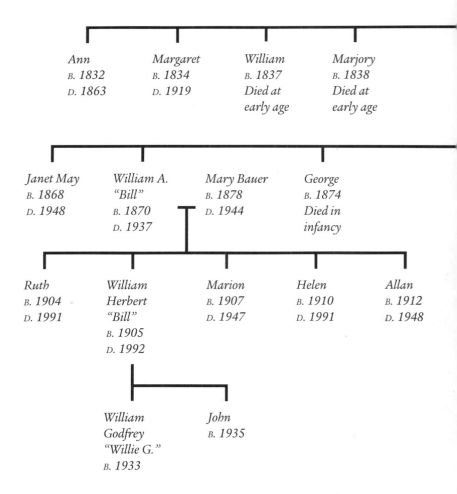

Ann	Margaret	William	Marjory
B. 1832	B. 1834	B. 1837	B. 1838
D. 1863	D. 1919	Died at early age	Died at early age

Janet May	William A. "Bill"	Mary Bauer	George
B. 1868	B. 1870	B. 1878	B. 1874
D. 1948	D. 1937	D. 1944	Died in infancy

Ruth	William Herbert "Bill"	Marion	Helen	Allan
B. 1904	B. 1905	B. 1907	B. 1910	B. 1912
D. 1991	D. 1992	D. 1947	D. 1991	D. 1948

William Godfrey "Willie G."	John
B. 1933	B. 1935

Note: *This family tree only shows Davidson family members who are mentioned in this book.*

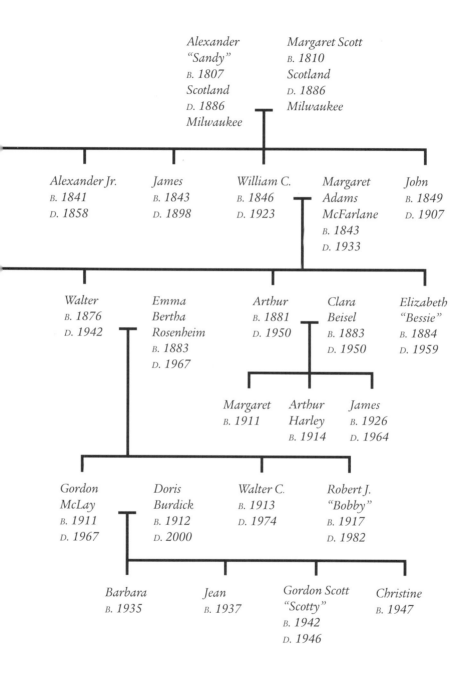

Alexander
"Sandy"
B. 1807
Scotland
D. 1886
Milwaukee

Margaret Scott
B. 1810
Scotland
D. 1886
Milwaukee

Alexander Jr.
B. 1841
D. 1858

James
B. 1843
D. 1898

William C.
B. 1846
D. 1923

Margaret
Adams
McFarlane
B. 1843
D. 1933

John
B. 1849
D. 1907

Walter
B. 1876
D. 1942

Emma
Bertha
Rosenheim
B. 1883
D. 1967

Arthur
B. 1881
D. 1950

Clara
Beisel
B. 1883
D. 1950

Elizabeth
"Bessie"
B. 1884
D. 1959

Margaret
B. 1911

Arthur
Harley
B. 1914

James
B. 1926
D. 1964

Gordon
McLay
B. 1911
D. 1967

Doris
Burdick
B. 1912
D. 2000

Walter C.
B. 1913
D. 1974

Robert J.
"Bobby"
B. 1917
D. 1982

Barbara
B. 1935

Jean
B. 1937

Gordon Scott
"Scotty"
B. 1942
D. 1946

Christine
B. 1947

Harley–Davidson Motorcycling Timeline

1901: Twenty-one-year-old William S. Harley and his childhood chum, twenty-year-old Arthur Davidson, start dreaming of and then designing a single-cylinder motorcycle. George M. Hendee's Hendee Mfg. Co. of Springfield, Massachusetts, offers its first Indian "motocycle," engineered by Oscar Hedstrom.

1902: Joe Merkel launches his Merkel motorcycle from the Milwaukee-based Merkel Motor Company.

1903: Walter Davidson is enlisted by Arthur Davidson and Bill Harley to assemble the first Harley-Davidson prototype, which is then taken for its first ride. The famous shed is built, and sister Janet Davidson names the "company" by painting on the door: "HARLEY DAVIDSON MOTOR CO." Three Harley-Davidson "motor-bicycles" are built.

1904: After the maid robs the fledgling company of its savings, the Davidson boys' hermit uncle James McLay comes to the rescue by loaning them his life savings. Three more motorcycles are built and sold, and the "factory" is expanded with an addition to the shed.

1905: The first employee is hired, and seven motorcycles are built.

1907: The Harley-Davidson Motor Company is incorporated. Walter Davidson is named president; Bill Harley is chief engineer and treasurer; Arthur Davidson is secretary and general sales manager; William A. Davidson is works manager.

1908: Walter Davidson wins the Federation of American Motorcyclists (FAM) Endurance Run in the Catskill Mountains.

1909: Bill Harley unveils his first 45-degree 61-ci V-twin by grafting a second cylinder onto his existing single.

1910: Harley-Davidson now employs 149 workers.

1914: Goaded by Indian's racing success at the Milwaukee motordrome, Bill Harley establishes the company's first official Racing Department. With 1,570 employees at the factory, Harley-Davidson builds 16,284 motorcycles.

1916: The U.S. Army conscripts Harley-Davidson motorcycles as cavalry mounts to chase after Mexican revolutionary "Pancho" Villa. *The Enthusiast* owner's magazine is launched.

1917: Establishment of the Harley-Davidson Service School. The company introduces a full line of bicycles.

1917–1918: During World War I, the Allies are armed with more than 20,000 Harley-Davidsons.

1918: Harley-Davidson boasts more than 2,000 dealers around the world, from Tasmania to Europe, Japan to Iceland.

"The World's Champion Motorcycle"
The sign above the door said it all at J. H. Hull's early dealership. (Bruce Davidson Collection)

1920: Harley-Davidson is the largest motorcycle maker in the world, both in factory floor space and number of machines produced.

1929: The Great Depression erupts with the stock market crash on Black Tuesday, October 29, 1929. The WL 45-ci sidevalve model is unveiled.

1931: Three-wheeled Servi-Car introduced.

1933: Total U.S. motorcycle production plummets from 32,000 cycles annually during the late 1920s to just 6,000 by 1933. Harley-Davidson builds just 3,700 motorcycles this year.

1935: The Model 61 OHV "Knucklehead" is first shown to dealers—although it will be months before the model is widely available.

1936: Six sons of the founders are working at the factory: Walter Davidson's sons Gordon and Walter C.; William Davidson's sons William Herbert and Allan; and Bill Harley's sons William J. and John.

1937: Founder William A. Davidson dies.

1939: World War II is sparked, and Harley-Davidson receives its first order for 5,000 military motorcycles from Great Britain.

1941–1946: During World War II, Harley-Davidson builds 88,000 military cycles, most of them the 45-ci WLA and WLC models.

1942: Harley-Davidson founder and President Walter Davidson dies in February. From his deathbed, he names his nephew William H. as the new president, and his own eldest son, Gordon, as vice president of manufacturing.

1943: Founder William S. Harley dies.

1947: Media hype surrounding a fracas on the Fourth of July at Hollister, California, inspires public fear of a new type of outlaw, the biker.

1948: A revised and refined version of the 61- and 74-ci Knucklehead arrives with the moniker "Panhead."

1950: Founder Arthur Davidson dies.

1952: The K-model is introduced as a lightweight, sports machine; it evolves in 1957 into the Sportster.

1953: Harley-Davidson celebrates its fiftieth anniversary. Indian builds its last Chief motorcycle. *The Wild One* debuts with Marlon Brando on a Triumph Thunderbird and Lee Marvin as the "bad" outlaw biker on a Harley-Davidson.

1961: Harley-Davidson becomes majority owner of Aermacchi motorcycles of Italy and begins importing the lightweight machines into the United States.

1962: Harley-Davidson unveils its new golf cart line.

1964: The Hell's Angels are catapulted into the national spotlight following a wild beach-party brouhaha over Labor Day weekend near Big Sur, California.

1965: Harley-Davidson goes public. The Bangor Punta Corp. attempts a hostile takeover. Dawn of the "Shovelhead" engine. Harley-Davidson first offers an "electric leg"—an electric starter—on the Electra-Glide.

1966: Brigitte Bardot has a hit with the Serge Gainsbourg–penned song "Harley-Davidson," featuring the statement: "I don't need anyone else on my Harley-Davidson"

1968: Harley-Davidson's board of directors recommends selling the company to Outboard Marine Corp., but OMC declines. In late 1968, the directors then recommend selling to American Machine and Foundry (AMF). Harley-Davidson produces only 15,475 motorcycles.

1969: Harley-Davidson is sold to AMF in January 1969. Bill Davidson stays on as president under AMF's control. *Easy Rider* opens with Peter Fonda as Captain America and Dennis Hopper as Billy setting off across America on their "chopped" Harleys.

1970: A motorcycle daredevil by the name of Evel Knievel joins forces with Harley-Davidson and begins performing stunts on an XR-750.

1971: Designer Willie G. Davidson's first factory custom, the FX Superglide, debuts with a patriotic red-white-and-blue paint scheme.

1973: Motorcycle assembly moved from the venerable Milwaukee factory to a new facility in York, Pennsylvania.

1974: Evel Knievel attempts to jump Idaho's Snake River Canyon with his jet-powered "SkyCycle." Robert M. Pirsig's *Zen and the Art of Motorcycle Maintenance* published.

1981: The famous Harley-Davidson buy-back takes place on June 16, 1981, with Willie G. Davidson along with AMF's Vaughn Beals, Harley-Davidson President Charles Thompson, and several others purchasing the company.

1984: Launch of the new aluminum Evolution V^2 engine, sometimes known as the "Blockhead."

1994: Harley-Davidson files with the U.S. Patent and Trademark Office to register the sound of its V-twin engine as a trademark. Harley's trademark attorney, Joseph Bonk, compared the sound to a spud, stating that the idle sounds like *"potato–potato–potato."*

1998: Harley-Davidson buys majority ownership in ex-Harley designer Erik Buell's sportbike-building firm and plans a full line of innovative Harley-powered café racers.

1999: Harley-Davidson engineers introduce the Twin Cam 88, nicknamed the "Fathead."

2001: Harley-Davidson celebrates 100 years since William Harley and Arthur Davidson began work on their motorcycle prototype.

Chapter 1

From Scotland to Wisconsin

The year was 1858, and the Davidson family of Scotland was setting sail across the Atlantic Ocean to a strange new country, America. My great-great-grandfather, Alexander "Sandy" Davidson, his wife, Margaret Scott, and their six children were immigrating to the United States to start a new life.

Making the decision to leave their beloved homeland must have been heartbreaking. The Scots were known the world over for being a hardy group who loved their country, where family roots were deeply entrenched and where each person belonged to a clan. Sandy was proud to be a part of the Davidson clan, which had stayed together through good times and bad. He was an established carpenter in the village of Brechin and was well known for his creative and artistic ability, and he took great pride in his original ideas. At age fifty-one, he knew it would be a challenge to re-establish himself in a foreign country.

Margaret's mother and other relatives were already living in America and wrote glowing letters of their new home. These letters told of a better life where conditions were not as harsh, and prosperity was yours if you worked hard. Sandy knew he was a hard worker, so if going to America would give his children a chance for a better life, he would do it. Besides, one of the couple's children, Alexander Jr., was recognized as a scholar with great potential.

Alexander "Sandy" and Margaret Scott
Davidson, 1858

Amidst sad farewells, the family packed their few possessions and boarded a boat bound for America. Excitement was in the air. The Davidson family had never traveled before, and now they were venturing forth on a life-changing journey. There must have been times on this scary voyage when they were tempted to change their minds and return home, but then they reminded themselves they were headed to the great land of opportunity.

There was great sadness on this trip as well. On the way across the Atlantic, Alexander Jr., the child with the bright future, contracted ship's fever. He died shortly after arriving on the shores of America.

The family's destination was the village of Winneconne, Wisconsin, where Margaret's relatives had settled. Unbeknownst to Sandy and Margaret Davidson, Winneconne was the true American frontier, an Indian village populated at times by members of several different tribes, including the Sauk, Fox, Chippewa/Ojibwe, and Menominee. Located in the heart of Wisconsin, the Wolf River flows through the town from the north, widening into two large lakes, Poygan and Winneconne. After the European settlers arrived, the village became a logging center. When Margaret's relatives came from Scotland, they were some of the first Europeans to settle there, starting the town's general store and a Presbyterian church. Sandy's family moved in with them, and through tears and laughter, stories were exchanged of their homeland and this new land.

After a short time, Sandy found work as a carpenter with the Chicago, Milwaukee & St. Paul Railroad, which required him to pack up his family and move first to Portage, Wisconsin, and then on to Milwaukee.

Adjusting to their new surroundings was a different experience for each one of them. Margaret was an outgoing person who enjoyed social activities and made friends easily. Sandy had a harder time: He was reserved and preferred being alone. But when they saw the rolling hills and many lakes around Milwaukee, they were both happy, for it reminded them of their beloved Scotland.

By the time Sandy and Margaret settled in Milwaukee, they considered themselves fortunate to have their five remaining children: Ann, Margaret, James, William C. (my great-grandfather), and John. Ann would marry Alexander McNab, who owned the Linen & Fancy Works store in Milwaukee. She enjoyed only five years in America before dying at a young age after the birth of her second child. Maggie, her sister, never married and took on the role of caring for Ann's husband and children. James suffered inflammatory rheumatism and heart disease, depending on his mother to take care of him throughout his fifty-five years. John, the youngest son, owned a mill outside of Milwaukee, where he accidentally drowned. Sandy and Margaret never complained of their losses but were thankful for their blessings. One of these blessings was watching their son William C. follow in his father's footsteps.

William C. inherited the gift of creativity from his father: He too loved to design and build things with his own hands. Because of this, he chose to follow his father and became a carpenter by trade. Working for the Chicago, Milwaukee & St. Paul Railroad as Sandy did enabled William C. to learn both on the job and at home. As a hobby, he built furniture and cabinets, and Milwaukee people who wanted quality work began to come to William C. with orders. Known to many as a quiet, dour Scot, he also preferred to be alone, dreaming and planning out new and original things to create.

When he decided to marry, William C. courted an outgoing Scot girl named Margaret Adams McFarlane who lived in the small Scottish settlement in Cambridge, Wisconsin. The McFarlane clan chose Cambridge because, like other early immigrants, they wanted to settle in an area that reminded them of their homeland and stay close to one another to reinforce their heritage. Margaret was loved and respected by her community and church; with her kind-spirited way, she was always ready and willing to help others. Her community would sadly miss her cheery smile and gracious behavior if she married this young Davidson lad from Milwaukee. But love is strong! Packing her belongings, she said goodbye to family and friends and moved to Milwaukee to become part of the Davidson clan. Because family ties were so important to Scottish families, she often returned home to visit Cambridge. Many years later, William C. acquired property on Lake Ripley outside of Cambridge so their children could spend summers with their relatives.

Upon arriving in Milwaukee in 1870, Margaret was warmly welcomed into the Davidson clan, which was living at 572 9th street. They all lived together until 1874 when William C. rented a home at 232 9th Street for his growing family. Living within blocks of other family members, Margaret felt she was in another community of relatives who were always there for each other. Deeply religious, she became one of the earliest members of the Calvary Presbyterian Church. Margaret was always a gracious hostess, and many relatives from Cambridge would stay in the Davidson home while visiting Milwaukee. And, as would have happened in Scotland, the two clans of Davidson and McFarlane became closely knit.

It was at the modest Milwaukee home of the Davidson family that motorcycling history would be made.

Chapter 2

Two Boys with a Dream

William C. and Margaret Davidson bought a home in 1897 on the outskirts of Milwaukee at 315 37th Street, on the northwestern corner of 37th and Highland, that would have room to raise a family. Like his father, William C. worked long hours in the railroad's carpentry shop, but in his spare time, he was in his home's basement crafting furniture. Margaret was renowned for keeping a spotlessly clean home. Together, they raised their five children: Janet May, William A., Walter (my grandfather), Arthur, and Elizabeth, better known as "Bessie." Middle initials were used to differentiate the different Williams and other Davidsons who shared names across generations; the initials usually did not stand for any name, and none of the other children had middle initials. Eventually, all of the children at one time or another became involved with their youngest brother's dream of making a motorcycle. It truly did become a family affair.

Arthur's childhood chum was William Sylvester Harley, who had been the family's next-door neighbor when they lived on 9th Street. Everyone called him, simply and fondly, Bill. The boys were always together, both in and out of school. They were smitten by the blossoming age of technology and dreamed of creating new motorized inventions. When school was out for the day, they would head straight to the Davidson basement and try to

Chicago, Milwaukee & St. Paul Railroad Carpentry Shop, 1869

William C. Davidson (third from right) worked as a carpenter in the railroad shops, as did his father, Alexander. The promise of a job in the railroad shop is what brought Alexander and the Davidson clan to Milwaukee in the first place. William C.'s sons William A. and Walter also worked for the railroad as young men, where William A. was known to fabricate motorcycle parts on the company's machine tools. Railroad old-timers joked that much of the first Harley-Davidsons were built in the railroad shops.

turn their ideas into reality, working in the carpentry workshop of William C.

Bill Harley's parents had emigrated from Littleport, England, a town about seventy-five miles north of London. His mother and my great-grandmother were neighbors who became best friends. Bill was born in 1880 in the United States. He had five younger siblings who all died; he and his older sister were the only surviving children.

Bill Harley was one year older than Arthur Davidson, but they became inseparable. They were always trying out new schemes together, and what one didn't think of, the other one did. Arthur didn't like to go to school, and his mother was constantly trying to keep him attending. He was always too busy plotting new projects to bother with staying in school.

When they weren't trying to build some new mechanical creation, the duo grabbed their fishing poles and headed for the lake to pursue their favorite pastime of fishing. Because the roads were muddy and full of ruts, it took the avid young fishermen longer than they liked to get to their favored fishing hole. As they impatiently pedaled their bicycles, they naturally started thinking of ways to speed up the trip to the fishing spot. That desire prompted them in 1900 to start dreaming of a way to add motors onto their bicycles. There was no plan to revolutionize the world with motorized transportation or earn their fortunes. Arthur Davidson and Bill Harley simply thought that if they could design and build a "motor-bicycle," it would serve two purposes: They could get to the fishing hole faster while having fun on the way.

Working was a way of life for young people in the early 1900s. Tinkering in the basement was frowned upon because it was seen as just a hobby and not a way to make a living. Both boys needed to work to help support their families, so they applied and got jobs at the Barth Manufacturing Company in Milwaukee, which specialized in metal fabricating. Soon

William C. and Margaret Davidson, late 1800s

moving on from the Barth firm, the duo worked at Pawling & Harnischfeger, the world-famous maker of mining equipment. At P&H, Arthur was an apprentice pattern maker and Bill an apprentice draftsman. But during their lunch breaks and on the way home, they still talked about their dream of making a motorized bicycle.

In 1895, an inventor-promoter from Indiana named Edward Pennington crafted a compact gasoline engine that he fitted into the rear frame section of a bicycle and called it a "motor cycle." Pennington brought his creation to Milwaukee to show it off that same year. There was a lot of publicity, and large crowds came to see him ride it down Wisconsin Avenue. This was not far from where Arthur and Bill lived, so I am sure that if it were at all possible they were in that crowd watching and marveling at someone going fifty-eight miles per hour on a motorized bicycle. Arthur would have been fourteen years old and Bill fifteen—just the age for dreams to get started.

One night several years later, Arthur and Bill went to the Bijou Theater to see a Parisian-born comedienne named Anna Held. Straight from Paris's famous Folies Bergère, she opened her show by whizzing across the stage on a nickel-plated French motor-bicycle. Arthur and Bill looked not only at this shapely damsel in white tights, but they also couldn't take their eyes off of the machine she was riding. The French motor-bicycle spurred on their dreams.

The next day, while at work at Barth Manufacturing, the duo told fellow workers all about the show, the French motor-bicycle, and how they were trying to build such a machine themselves. One of their fellow workers stepped forward and said he thought he could help them. His name was Emil Kroeger, and he was a German-born mechanic who was familiar with Count Albert de Dion's pioneering single-cylinder, internal-combustion, gasoline-fueled, four-stroke engine that was widely used in Europe. Arthur and Bill became good friends with Emil, sharing the problems they were having with their motor design. Emil offered his knowledge of the de Dion engine, and the boys' enthusiasm reached a new level. They couldn't get to the family basement fast enough to try out their ideas. Their fascination with motors was becoming a reality, thanks to their newfound friend.

Like all inventions, nothing came easily. They did not have any engineering books to guide them, so everything was done by trial and error. Not having any specialized tools, they utilized whatever was available. They worked and reworked their plans, always thinking of something new to try.

During summers when school was out, Bill Harley worked at the Meiselbach Bicycle factory in Milwaukee and came to know the ins and outs of bicycle construction. Being familiar with frames, Bill knew that a standard "diamond-shaped" bicycle frame was too flimsy to carry a motor. Their goal was to design a new frame that could accommodate their engine. Eventually, they created a "loop" frame that worked so well they continued to use the design for decades. Nothing was fancy, for money was limited.

By 1902, there were a handful of motorcycles on the city's streets made by a variety of builders. On Milwaukee's south side, a man named Joe Merkel was building his Merkel motorcycles at the Merkel Motor Company. The first Merkel was a typical motor bicycle with a diamond-style bicycle frame fitted with a single-cylinder engine and a leather belt driving the rear wheel. By 1903, Merkel had given up on the diamond frame and created a loop frame. Bill and Arthur decided they should look at how someone else conceived of a motorcycle, so they watched and studied Joe Merkel's inventions. Eventually the boys decided they could make a better machine.

Help came from friends and family when they least expected it. William C. had many carpentry tools but not always the ones they needed. An acquaintance named Henry Melk lived down

Ole Evinrude and Arthur Davidson, 1902

Ole Evinrude (center top) and Arthur (bottom) pose in 1902 within the spokes of a pattern made by their jointly owned pattern-making company. The other two men were employees at the firm. (Arthur H. Davidson Collection)

the block and had a lathe in his basement. He allowed Arthur and Bill to come over at night to machine components for their motors.

During the summer months, Arthur went to stay with his grandmother on her farm in Cambridge. There he met another boy named Ole Evinrude who became a best buddy. Born in Norway, Ole was three years older than Arthur and had considerably more worldly experience. He studied books on gasoline engineering and was also experimenting with motors. Like Arthur, Ole too was a dreamer, at work on his own invention of a carburetor design for outboard boat motors. When Arthur and Bill later crafted a primitive carburetor for their motorcycle engine using a tomato-soup can as the throttle body, they had problems getting the fuel flow right. It was Ole who offered his help in perfecting the first Harley-Davidson carburetor.

Ole and Arthur chummed around together during the summer months, always tinkering with new ideas and reinforcing each other's fascination with motors. Cambridge is situated on Lake Ripley, so Ole and Arthur fished whenever they could. Neither of them liked the idea of having to row their boat to get to the good fishing spots, which started them thinking about adapting a motor to power a rowboat.

Arthur and Ole spent many weekends together discussing the problems each one was tackling. Because they both loved to create casting patterns, Ole and Arthur eventually started their own small pattern-making company together.

Even though they were only in their twenties, they liked to tell each other how successful each would be some day. They were so positive of this that they made a pact stating neither one would ever compete with the other. As time has shown, Arthur and Ole never did try to branch into one another's business. By 1903, Ole had started two companies, the Clemick-Evinrude Company, which was a pattern maker and engine builder, and the Motor Car Power Equipment Company. Ole's later Evinrude Company became famous for its Elto and Evinrude outboard motors at the same time as the Harley-Davidson Motor Company became renowned for its motorcycles. Arthur and Ole stayed close friends, always joking about their pact and how they honored it throughout the years.

By 1903, Arthur was twenty-two and Bill was twenty-three years old, and they had been working and reworking their idea of a motorcycle for three years. Arthur later remembered people advising them to quit their dreaming, telling them, "Come on boys, life is based on hard work. Wasting your time dreaming is not going to get you anywhere. Be thankful you have jobs with wages. Hard work is the key to success for immigrant families, and tinkering in a basement is *not* hard work." Fortunately, they didn't listen.

Arthur's father and grandfather, being artistic dreamers themselves, were more understanding. They looked kindly on the pair, remembering how they felt when they dreamed up ideas and tried to make them work. Yet Arthur had another gift that his father and grandfather did not possess: He had the wonderful gift of being a talker, like his mother. He was a natural-born salesman who would tell anyone and everyone about his dreams.

What made this dream of building a motorcycle different was that Arthur and Bill's enthusiasm didn't die but kept getting stronger with each part they perfected. The Davidson basement was filling with patterns and components that changed continually with each new adjustment. Finally, the duo felt they had produced the right parts with the right patterns. As they started putting their first motorcycle together, my grandfather told us decades later, they were already thinking about how much fun they were going to have getting to their favorite fishing holes. After much time and frustration, however, they realized that no matter how hard they tried, they could not figure out how to assemble the parts into a working machine. They started thinking that they should sell all the parts as a mail-order kit and let the buyer put it together. But if they couldn't do it, how could a buyer?

So, with parts scattered all around the basement floor, it was time to call for help. What they needed was a top-notch mechanic, but the only one they knew was Arthur's older brother, Walter. Unfortunately, he was working as a machinist for the Missouri, Kansas & Texas Railroad in Parsons, Kansas. As luck had it, Walter and Arthur's older brother, William A., was soon to be married to Mary Bauer, and Walter would be coming home to Milwaukee for the wedding. What perfect timing! Why not send him a letter inviting him to take a ride on their new invention? Walter wrote back saying, yes, he was looking forward to this ride. He had been hearing about their new-fangled invention for the last two years, so he was curious to see what Arthur and Bill had put together. Of course, they neglected to tell him that first he would have to assemble all the parts.

When Walter saw what was spread out all over his parents' basement, he wasn't the least bit discouraged. He liked putting things together and felt right at home. He set to work, and as soon as he finished, he jumped on this forerunner of their famous motorcycle and took the first ride. The motor sputtered to life but wasn't powerful enough to make it up any hills. Still, that ride would change all of their lives.

Walter became so enthused with the motor-bicycle that he quit his job in Kansas and moved back into the family home. He quickly took a job with the same railroad as his father and brother William A. Living at home, Arthur, Walter, and Bill Harley could spend all of their spare time working on improving their creation.

Now that Walter had joined the team, the thought of selling the motorized bike as a mail-order kit ended, replaced by the idea of designing and producing a finished product. Each young man developed his individual talent. Arthur Davidson was the pattern maker. Bill Harley was the draftsman. Walter joined them as machinist and skilled mechanic. Each one kept his full-time job but devoted all his spare time to perfecting their dream machine. They were getting closer to rolling the first production Harley-Davidson motorcycle out the door.

Walter Davidson, 1903

Chapter 3

Out of the Basement and into the Shed

My great-grandmother Margaret Davidson was famed far and wide for keeping a neat house. It was one thing having Arthur and his pal Bill Harley tracking dirt and grease in and out all the time, but now Walter had moved back home to join them in their venture. Many nights, their father, William C. looked forward to spending some time alone working on his carpentry, but would find his grease-caked sons and the neighbor boy noisily hammering out their invention. It didn't take long for the basement to get crowded with the Davidson boys, Bill Harley, and William C. all working on projects.

Margaret could not stand it any longer. My grandfather Walter used to tell the story to us grandchildren about the day his mother stormed up to William C. and hotly laid down the law: "You will have to do something about all this mess in the basement! It is one thing to have you down there building furniture but another to have our two sons and their friend Bill tracking dirt and grease into our house. I won't put up with this any longer!"

William agreed with her. Even though he approved of the boys' project, he also liked to keep the peace.

Harley-Davidson "Factory," 1903
Sketch by William McLay Oeflein of the famous shed built in 1903 behind the Davidson family's house at 38th and Highland. William Oeflein is the great-great-grandson of William C. Davidson.

The next day, he bought a supply of used lumber and built a ten-by-fifteen-foot shed in the backyard. Now the young men had their own workshop. I can just picture my great-grandmother shaking her finger at her sons, saying, "Take all your parts and patterns to the shed! I will not have this mess in my basement any longer!"

Now everyone was happy. Margaret could keep her house neat, William C. could go down into his basement and work in peace on his furniture, and the young inventors could go out into their own shed and make all the noise they needed.

What the fledgling motorcyclists really needed were more machine tools. Henry Melk down the street came to the rescue by selling William C. his used lathe, which was powered by a cantankerous gasoline engine. This engine would quit running exactly when it was needed the most.

The rest of the Davidson family soon was drawn into the dream. Janet Davidson, the oldest sister in the family, was also creative and loved to work with her hands. Today, she probably would have been out there with her brothers wrenching on the motorcycle, but back in the early 1900s, it just wasn't very lady-like. Her uncle, Alexander McNab, owned a linen store, so she went to work for him and took advantage of her artistic talent by designing original monograms for fine linens. Janet liked

45

Janet Davidson Lettering the Harley-Davidson Logo, 1903

Drawing of Janet, the elder sister of the Davidson boys, hand-painting the Harley-Davidson lettering on an early motorcycle. This drawing was created by artist Paul Smith, who is most noted for creating Harley-Davidson's graphic with the eagle atop the bar-and-shield logo, which first appeared on the 1976 Liberty Edition models honoring the American bicentennial.

the work, especially when customers asked specifically for her artistry in design. When her father built the shed for her brothers, she could not resist adding her own touch. Finding a can of paint, she hand-painted the letters on the door: "HARLEY DAVIDSON MOTOR CO."

Janet also began work on designing a logo for the boys. A short time later when the first motorcycles rolled out the door, Janet was out in the shed hand-painting the logo on the tanks and painting red pinstriping on each tank and fender. She was proud to be able to contribute her artistic touch to the boys' dream.

The eldest of the Davidson sons, William A., was six years older than my grandfather Walter and eleven years older than Arthur. His mechanical education took place in the machine shops of the Chicago, Milwaukee & St. Paul Railroad where, at the age of sixteen, he started swinging a hammer. With a reputation of being a hard-working, responsible young man, it wasn't long before he was promoted to toolroom foreman. At his wedding, he heard talk of the mysterious motorcycle ride that his brother Walter was going to take. When Walter quit his well-paying job in Kansas to join in his younger brother's venture, William A. also became enamored by the idea of a motor-bicycle. He had plenty of time to find out more during the Davidson clan Sunday dinners. William A. and his new wife, Mary, were invited over every Sunday, and each time they visited, he became more and more interested in what was going on, first in the basement and then in the shed. He yearned to join them, but being married and starting a family of his own was a serious undertaking.

Whereas Arthur, Walter, and Bill Harley were still bachelors living at home and spending all their time working on their dream machine, William A. helped by being a good listener and making suggestions on ways to improve the parts. He became

1905

The Future of Transportation, 1905

An unidentified man kneels down to examine the engine on an early Harley-Davidson parked in front of the shed. (State Historical Society of Wisconsin/ WHI (X3) 14799)

THE HARLEY-DAVIDSON DEALER

MAKES CLAIM OF RECORD

Stephen E. Sparough's 1903 Harley-Davidson Has Covered 83,000 Miles and Is Anxious for More.

That Harley-Davidson machines give good service year after year is shown by the letter on the opposite page received by C. H. Lang, Chicago dealer.

Steve J. Sparough, an expert repairman employed by the Thomas B. Jeffery company, boasts a 1903 Harley-Davidson machine that has made 83,000 miles and that is good for many more thousands of miles.

The 3¼ horsepower motor is still in perfect condition. At the earnest solicitation of Mr. Lang the old-timer was permitted by Mr. Sparough to visit its birthplace.

What it saw there is a remarkable story—as remarkable as the performance of this old veteran of the city pavement and the country road—and would well merit the attention of any good biographer.

HIS HARLEY-DAVIDSON IS ALWAYS READY WHEN HE WANTS IT.

Claim to Fame, 1912
The Harley-Davidson Dealer *was proud to feature this early 1903 model and its stellar service history.*

Factory Addition, 1904
Sketch by William McLay Oeflein of the first addition to the original shed, which was added in 1904.

the one they would consult whenever they ran into a problem. He also became the one who would lend a helping hand when they needed it most. After Arthur made new patterns based on Bill Harley's drawings, William A. would often take the patterns to the railroad toolroom and surreptitiously fabricate them on the railroad's professional machines. Many old-time Milwaukee railroad workers joked for years afterward about how much of the first Harley-Davidson motorcycles came out of the railroad shops.

What's in a name? Why the name Harley-Davidson? Why not Davidson-Harley? I have been asked this question my whole life. I know that my father and all of the family members involved with Harley-Davidson have been asked this question as well.

Surprisingly, perhaps, there is no one answer to this query. Yet there have been numerous stories that I have heard passed down through the years speculating on the origin of the name's order.

Some family members say that because there was only one Harley and he was always at the Davidson home surrounded by the large Davidson clan, the founders thought they would put Bill Harley's name first out of pure politeness and good manners as hosts. That's one theory.

Another story goes that because there was just the two of them in the beginning—Arthur Davidson and Bill Harley—and since Harley, being one year older, was the senior of the two, his name went first.

Yet another story states that since Bill Harley drew the plans, he was more important in the creation of the motorcycle than Arthur, who made the patterns. So, Harley's name came first. Yet knowing something about the character of Bill Harley and Arthur Davidson, I doubt one thought he was more important than the other; they would not have stayed best friends their whole lives if that was true. They each had a unique gift that each developed to the fullest, and one could not have done it without the other. Thus, I have my doubts about this version.

Here are my thoughts on the subject. There were two best friends with a dream. They had no idea that their invention would become a worldwide icon. Like best friends everywhere, they did not care whose name was first. "Harley-Davidson" simply flowed off of the tongue better than "Davidson-Harley." When you name your children, you pick the name that sounds the best.

I am sure when Janet painted those letters on the shed door, she was doing it in jest as an older sister who was just trying to make her little brothers working on their dream feel important.

When the first Harley-Davidson motorcycle rolled forth from the shed behind the Davidson house in 1903, the boys were in good company with other inventors. The same year also witnessed Orville and Wilbur Wright's first motorized flight. New ideas and inventions were popping up everywhere: Alexander Graham Bell's telephone, Albert Einstein's General Theory of Relativity, and Thomas Elva Edison's 1,000 patents covering everything from incandescent lights to phonographs to motion pictures led the way. In the motoring world, George Hendee and Oscar Hedstrom were developing the Indian "motocycle" in Springfield, Massachusetts, and a man named Henry Ford was starting an automobile company in Dearborn, Michigan. The times were certainly changing.

By the end of 1903, three complete Harley-Davidson motorcycles had been built and assembled by hand on weekends and at night. All three of the first Harley-Davidsons were sold immediately, the first one going to the boys' friend, Henry Meyer, who was notorious for hating to walk to work. He loved having something new and unusual, and motored all over town so he could show off his purchase.

The roads in those days were nothing like today's roads. While some of the streets in Milwaukee were made of brick or cobblestones, most of them were dirt paths pocked by ruts. In the country, the roads followed animal paths, horse trails, and wagon tracks. One can only imagine the muddy mess these roads became when it rained or snowed and how difficult it was to get anywhere. When people saw the first Harley-Davidson motorcycle pass by on these roads, they were more curious than impressed. To most folk, the thought of traveling around on one of these motorized bikes seemed dangerous, impractical, and even inappropriate.

How could these young founders prove their motorcycle was an economical and safe way to travel? Arthur pondered this issue for days. If they could show people how much less work a motorcycle was than a horse and carriage, they could sell them on the practicality. It didn't take long to convince the people who used horses because they already knew how much time was spent keeping a horse healthy and productive.

There was also another new form of transportation around town. Automobiles were starting to be used as an efficient form of transportation, but their price was still beyond the reach of most middle-class Americans.

Knowing these things, my grandfather told me their plan: "Let's price our motorcycles at $200 and advertise them as a form of reliable and economic transportation." In the end, it worked, and they found themselves a market niche. More and more people came to want a Harley-Davidson motorcycle for everyday transportation.

It was important that the Harley-Davidson motorcycle be dependable because money was scarce and no one wanted to purchase something that needed to be fixed continually. In 1913, a company researcher traced the various owners of the first Harley-Davidson. It was first sold to Henry Meyer, who rode it

6,000 miles and then sold it to George Lyon, who put 15,000 more miles on it. The next three owners were Dr. Webster, Louis Fluke, and Stephen Sparrow. Between the three of them, another 62,000 miles of dependable travel was put on the bike. Not one of these owners ever had to replace the bearings. With this information, Harley-Davidson could advertise the dependability of their motorcycles. In 1913, an advertisement stated that the first Harley-Davidson motorcycle ever sold had covered more than 100,000 miles, was still operating, and still retained its original bearings.

A fabulous story of another one of the earliest Harley-Davidson motorcycles recently came to light. Through the years, an old Harley-Davidson has stood on display in the lobby of the main plant on Juneau Avenue. Dr. Martin Jack "Marty" Rosenblum, Harley-Davidson's archivist and historian, passed by it many times on his way to and from meetings and remembers having a feeling that there was something amiss. He asked permission to have this motorcycle disassembled to find out what was not right about it. Finally, in preparation for the 95th Harley-Davidson anniversary, he got the go-ahead. Ray Schlee, Harley-Davidson's professional restorer, was called in. Schlee was aided in his research on the bike by Rosenblum and outside experts Bruce Linsday and Mike Lange. To everyone's joy, it was documented as being serial number 1. The very first Harley-Davidson motorcycles built were not stamped with serial numbers; this was something the boys did later when production truly began. Thus, this was not the actual first Harley-Davidson but it was certainly one of the first, and may have been the first production motorcycle. Someone had changed the handlebars and the seat, but the frame and most of the rest of the motorcycle was original. It's exciting to think that this motorcycle made a full circle, starting its life in the shed behind my great-grandfather's home and is now preserved forever at the main plant on Juneau Avenue as a lasting treasure and remembrance to the founding fathers.

If this motorcycle could talk, it would undoubtedly have many stories to tell.

In 1904, the boys built and sold three more motorcycles. Bill Harley, age twenty-four, decided he wanted to learn as much as he could about internal-combustion engines. Packing an extra shirt and pocketing his meager savings, he traveled to Madison, Wisconsin, and enrolled in the University of Wisconsin to pursue an engineering degree. Even though he was eighty miles away, he came home as often as possible to help refine their dream machine.

At twenty-three years old, Arthur was the first to quit his outside job and become a full-time employee of the Harley-Davidson Motor Company. Soon his dream of getting to the fishing holes faster was replaced by just trying to find time to go fishing.

Arthur and Walter were living at home and spending all their spare time out in the shed. When they did come into the house, there was still a trail of grease and grime behind them. I can picture my grandmother shaking her head at the futility of it all and complaining, "You are always so dirty! Can't you just for once stay clean?"

Her words fell on deaf ears.

Chapter 4

The Honey Uncle to the Rescue

When orders for their motorcycles began coming their way, there were soon actual proceeds from the sales. Unaccustomed to having any extra money around, the boys didn't know what to do with the cash. They had no company bank account, so they employed an old canning jar as their "bank." For want of a place to keep this "bank," they hid it among the canned peaches and string beans in the Davidson house's pantry.

A story has been passed down in my family that my great-grandmother finally gave up in the battle to influence her sons to be cleaner and hired a maid to at least keep the house neat and tidy. It seemed this maid was doing a fine job—and also seemed to be living quite well. One day, my grandmother noticed how many trips the maid had been making to the pantry. Sure enough, when someone went to check on the "bank," the canning jar was empty. The maid had stolen all of the young company's earnings.

After this incident, any extra money was deposited in a true bank, and Bessie, the youngest member of the Davidson family, kept the company books. She had been watching the rest of her family become involved with this motorcycle business and wanted to help in whatever way she could. She was good with numbers and offered to keep all their financial records. She did this for many years, and in gratitude, her brothers later paid for her college education.

Like any young company, the boys were always in need of money—especially after the maid robbed the "bank." Today, they would probably go to a real bank and take out a venture-capital loan, but in those days that was not possible. People were too practical and worked too hard to hand over their meager savings to a few young men with a risky venture. The young men could only think of one way to keep their dream alive: door-to-door sales. Yes, each one would take his turn going door to door asking for money to invest in their motorcycles.

I remember decades later talking to a woman from Menominee Falls, Wisconsin, who recalled such a sales call: "When I was a young girl, there was a knock on our front door. I remember my father opening the door, and here was this young man asking if he could explain his dream of making motorcycles. He was very young, and my father listened to his plea for money to support his venture. Then my father laughed and slammed the door in his face, saying, 'Stop your foolish dreams and get a real job. Don't you know life is based on hard work. Time should not be wasted on dreams.'

"My father lived to see this young entrepreneur achieve his dream. He would retell this story many times through the years, wanting me to learn the valuable lesson of how I should always listen to people's ideas and not be quick to jump to conclusions."

Although most people did turn the boys down, a few listened to their plea and admired them for their dedication. Becoming enthused themselves, they donated money to keep these young men's dream alive. This extra money was used to produce more motorcycles and expand the shed in 1904 to a ten-by-thirty-foot "factory."

Each month more motorcycles rolled out the shed door. But by July 1904, the little motorcycle-manufacturing company had

AT
MILWAUKEE

Honey Uncle's Receipt, 1904
The receipt given to eighty-year-old hermit Uncle James MacLay in July 6, 1904.

Honey Uncle, 1904
Reclusive hermit James MacLay (standing) with his brother Moses visited family members in Milwaukee in 1904 and was intrigued by the motorcycle dreams of young Arthur, Walter, and Bill Harley. After the family's maid robbed the boys' "bank," the Honey Uncle loaned his life's savings to them, allowing them to keep the dream alive.

Harley-Davidson Employees and New Factory, 1907

With funds from the Honey Uncle's loan, the boys built this new factory in 1906—but then had to move it a foot and a half with help from these employees as it encroached on railroad property. The new factory was only a block away from the Davidson's residence. Over the years, many additions and new buildings would be added, and the property is still the current headquarters for Harley-Davidson.

outgrown its tiny shed and its addition. More space was needed. What could they do? They definitely did not have enough money to build a true factory. How could they let their dream die now, when there was such a demand for their product?

Just when things seemed hopeless, help arrived from a surprising source. The Davidson boys had a hermit uncle named James McLay who came to their rescue. James McLay was their mother's uncle, an eighty-year-old bachelor who lived a reclusive life in Madison on the now-famous Picnic Point of Lake Mendota. He had built himself a small cabin and enjoyed living alone, cut off from the world around him. He spent his time raising bees and living off the land. He cut out a slot in his front door for the barrel of his gun. Spreading grain on the path leading to his door, he would have a ready dinner when a squirrel, rabbit, or deer came to eat. He was a Scot, however, and never forgot his family ties, keeping in touch by writing letters on the backs of old calendars. Admiring people who followed their own dreams, he was always interested in the escapades of his young nephews and their crazy machine. Upon hearing of their financial dilemma, he decided to help them out by loaning them every penny of his life savings.

Needless to say, you can imagine how excited the young Davidsons were to receive such a windfall. With this money from Uncle James McLay, they purchased land down the hill from their home that was adjacent to the railroad tracks. Today, this site is still the company's permanent home although many additions and a newer factory have been built through the years.

Because of his contribution, James McLay was affectionately called the Honey Uncle. He was always honored and was paid back tenfold. It is said he came to the rescue because of his Scottish heritage and the importance of clans sticking together. My grandfather named his oldest son Gordon McLay (my father) after his Uncle James and would often tell the story of how this hermit relative came to the rescue when it was needed the most.

With the money from the Honey Uncle and new orders coming in, the boys were anxious to erect a new building. In 1906, they built their first building on what was then called Chestnut Street but was soon renamed Juneau Avenue. The new factory measured twenty-eight by eighty feet and seemed spacious in comparison with the old shed.

Being new in the building business, however, no one thought to survey the property lines. Sure enough, one day an agent for the railroad came and told them their new building was impinging on railroad property. Instead of calling in the lawyers like we would do today, my grandfather consulted their handful of employees. They all gathered outside and solved the problem in the most logical way: Together, they picked up the wood building, moved it a foot and a half off the railroad land, and went back to work. Everyone was happy.

Chapter 5

That Silent Gray Fellow

The boys had built three motorcycles in 1903 and another three in 1904. In 1905, they hired their first employee outside of their own group of founders, and with this extra pair of helping hands, the boys built an amazing seven machines that year. Five more employees were hired in 1906, and the production run skyrocketed to fifty motorcycles. In 1907, motorcycle production tripled to 150 machines. In 1908, another addition was made to the factory—this time measuring forty by sixty feet and built of long-lasting brick—and production nearly tripled again to 410 motorcycles. The boys' dream was now on a solid footing of bricks and mortar.

The first Harley-Davidson motorcycles were not flashy machines. Rather than being racers or speedsters, they became famous for being reliable motorcycles that would run forever. This was just the way the boys wanted them. Their engineering sense and the respect the motorcycles earned fit well with the boys' Scottish heritage, which stood strongly for the simple, practical, and sensible. I think it's fair to say that a Harley-Davidson motorcycle had a Scottish personality.

Motorcycles appealed to different types of riders. While racers wanted to compete in a sport that required special skills, and rebellious youth wanted to have something different from their peers, the majority of riders wanted an economical form

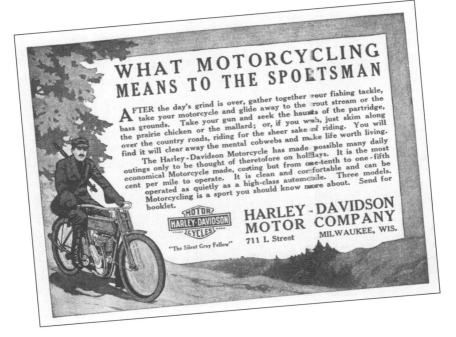

Fisherman On A Harley-Davidson, 1911

The company advertised its Silent Gray Fellow as being the ideal angler's ride: "After the day's grind is over, gather together your fishing tackle, take your motorcycle and glide away to the trout stream or the bass grounds."

of transportation that brought enjoyment along the way. The early Harley-Davidson was the motorcycle for the post carriers, police officers, delivery boys, farmhands, and commuters. It was a machine you could trust, a motorcycle you could always count on.

The boys' motorcycle was soon christened with the nickname "Silent Gray Fellow." The word "silent" was used because people wanted quiet transportation, a machine that would not scare horses or mules on the roads or startle folk in the streets. They wanted to relax to the soft hum of the engine subdued by a large muffler. The color gray was chosen because it was not flashy. Riders wanted their motorcycles to blend in with the environment and not stand out or be showy. The first Harley-Davidson motorcycles produced were painted black, but now Henry Ford was mass-producing horseless carriages, all in the color black, so Harley-Davidson picked gray as its own, unique color. And the name "fellow" was added to evoke in people the feeling of being able to get on their trusted friend and ride silently out into the country to enjoy the scenery. This motorcycle was designed to be a person's best friend.

I recently discovered a rare treasure from the past: my grandfather's personal, signed collection of *The Harley-Davidson Dealer*, the company dealer magazine that was published monthly in just 1912, 1913, and 1914. I sat and read through many articles and stories written by my grandfather, his brother Arthur, and Bill Harley. This story about a Harley-Davidson owner named J. W. Malte summed up how the motorcycle affected people's lives:

> I am a very quiet, uninteresting individual who works seven nights a week, every week, and has been doing so for longer than I like to remember. I have a pair of spectacles, a more or less exposed skypiece, and a lot of real experiences, most of which were both unpleasant and

Delivering a Motorcycle, 1906
Arthur (right) delivers an early Harley-Davidson to Cambridge, Wisconsin, postal carrier Pete Olson for use in mail delivery. Geo Keystin looks on. (Arthur E. Davidson Collection)

**Harley-Davidson
Employees, 1907**

unprofitable. I have not been promoted for so long, the edge of my ambition has been dulled, and for a year or two I have noticed I could not take an interest in my work I felt I should. I wanted to, all right, but somehow the resilient quality was gone. I was tired. I wanted to go somewhere and hear the birds sing; to just lie down on the grass and watch the clouds.

People told me I should take a lay off—that I was breaking down. But how could I take a lay off when my wages and the cost of living balanced almost to a penny? I might, but the grocery bill, the gas, water, clothes, and a hundred other bills would work over time. They don't belong to any union those bills don't.

By the way, did you ever see a 'Leven dollar bill'? I have and also Fifteen Dollar bills, Seventeen dollar bills, and all sorts of bills and I owed them all. No sir, there was no lay off for me. I just had to stick to the finish.

Last spring, I was feeling bad—all in—had about concluded that someone else could figure the cost of fuel, curse the smoke ordinance, and try to keep the wheels turning; when one morning as I was going home on the streetcar, I heard a man talking about motorcycles—that they did not cost much to buy, operate or maintain, were more convenient than an auto, and could be run at a very moderate cost.

'It was the poor man's friend', the man said. 'With one of them a tired working man could take a little run in the country any fine morning, fill himself with fresh air and never miss the time. They would add ten years to his life and 100 percent to his efficiency.'

That talk caught me. I rode five blocks past my corner to listen; went to bed and dreamed of riding along cool country roads watching the rabbits taking baths in the dust, of resting in the shadow of some mossy old

A Man and His Best Friend

With 120 miles to go to Denver, a rider had to rely on his Harley-Davidson in the days when roads were glorified farm trails.

bridge and maybe seeing the minnows darting about in the water below. In my dream I heard a sad call of the dove just as I used to hear it thirty years ago.

I awoke feeling better; life was not such a bad game after all. If a Phantom Cycle could put such a tingle in my blood, what would the Gasoline Wizard in fact instill?

I felt it was extravagance, but I must have it. The family objected. I could not ride a bicycle—how could I hope to ride one of those gasoline things, my family said. It was ridiculous at my age; could not afford it, they declared. One of my brothers promised to have an alienist look me over.

Nevertheless, I drew from the bank a big percent of savings of many paydays and exchanged it for a Harley-Davidson machine. Since then I have seen many motorcycles but to my mind none of them have as many likable qualities as my Harley-Davidson.

When I had gotten it home I felt very much like the little boy who has stolen his first kiss (somewhat embarrassed but awful glad). I won't say anything about my early efforts at riding. The weight of nearly 50 years did not help much. I will say that in a surprisingly short time I rode to work in or rather on my own machine and I know my work at the shop was better. I would take a little run in the country on my way home visiting places I had often wanted to see, talking to people far from the hum of our factory.

I was a Columbus, discovering new worlds every day, threw away pills and tonics and lived without effort. I was really alive again. I would go to bed full of pleasant things that I had seen and heard after riding my Harley-Davidson through the country roads. I had a new feeling of contentment.

This story was just one of many that I discovered in the pages of the different issues of *The Harley-Davidson Dealer*. People working long and hard hours would take their meager savings, purchase a Harley-Davidson motorcycle, and then have a whole new life, with the wind in their face and the freedom to explore the countryside. It sounds a lot like today.

Chapter 6

Racing to Compete

The founders of Harley-Davidson would have nothing to
do with motorcycle racing. They were inspired to build
their first motorcycle to carry them to the fishing hole,
and the early machines retained this practical, reliable, no-
nonsense personality. Racing was another world and a different temperament.

My grandfather Walter had that racing temperament, however. In fact, he was the only one of the founders who did. I can
just picture him saying to his brothers and Bill Harley, "Why
not try some racing? I'm still a bachelor without any responsi-
bilities to a wife and children. I think I can help our young company by making a name for our motorcycle in the racing world."
No one could argue with this logic—except maybe his mother,
who, like all mothers of racers everywhere, worried about her
child being injured.

As early as 1905, Walter was winning local race events aboard
a Harley-Davidson. In 1907, he won the Derby Day Races, the
Flying Start, and the Milwaukee Hillclimb. With these successes
under his belt, he started thinking about competing on the
National Circuit, where winning would bring great attention
to his machine.

In 1908, Walter packed up his Harley-Davidson and set off
to ride in the most grueling endurance race of that time, the
annual Federation of American Motorcyclists (FAM) Endurance
Run in the Catskill Mountains of upstate New York. This competition was a contest of endurance and skill, not speed and
daring. It covered 365 miles from the Catskills to New York City

Walter Davidson After Winning FAM Run, 1908
My grandfather Walter poses proudly with an early Harley-Davidson after winning the Federation of American Motorcyclists' Endurance Run with a perfect score.

by way of gravel and dirt roads, water crossings, and cow trails over treacherous mountains. It was a test of the abilities of each rider and his machine. Special tests were thrown in as surprises: Judges were hidden in bushes and behind trees along the route, ready to jump out in front of riders waving a green flag to signal an emergency brake test. And to add to the duress of the run, each checkpoint had to be reached exactly on time.

Of the sixty-one entrants in the FAM's 1908 Endurance Run,

my grandfather was the only rider on a Harley-Davidson. Since Harley-Davidson in the early years did not sponsor any racer or racing events, my grandfather was riding a stock machine without any special competition adaptations, and he was not backed by a company team or a squad of mechanics. Yet even though he felt alone and on his own, he was a perfectionist and knew his machine inside and out. He was confident in his ability to compete. As he told the Harley-Davidson faithful after the race, "So strong was my confidence that I carried with me no additional parts or repairs, which was quite in contrast with many of the manufacturers' riders who had automobiles with complete duplicate parts following them."

When the starting flag dropped at exactly six o'clock on the morning of June 29, 1908, my grandfather was ready. During the first day of this rugged course, fifteen riders washed out, but my grandfather passed through the checkpoints along the 175-mile-long trail without a hitch and finished the day with a perfect score.

The second day, Walter and the forty-three remaining riders covered the rugged 190 miles that circled around Long Island to Brooklyn. After the final flag waved, his performance was as flawless as it had been the day before.

Never before had any rider scored one perfect score—let alone two!—in this prestigious race. After checking his performance with the officials, the judges awarded Walter Davidson a unique winning score: a perfect 1,000 points plus an additional five merit points for outstanding consistency of both rider and machine. He was regaled with the coveted FAM diamond medal. "Davidson's title to the medal is beyond question," the FAM judges announced as if they didn't believe it themselves. "During the two days of the contest, he varied by eight minutes from the exact schedule, which places him so far in advance of all others as to leave his qualification for the award beyond dispute."

It was an auspicious beginning, to say the least.

With this win, the spotlight was on Harley-Davidson motorcycles, so Walter decided to try another race event. This one was an economy run in which each bike was tested on how far it could travel on a gallon of gas. Again, my grandfather finished ahead of everyone else with the top mark of 188 miles per gallon. With these two wins, people across the country began to sit up and take notice of the qualities of the Harley-Davidson.

Walter discovered he was a natural racer. As a perfectionist and as a full-fledged machinist/mechanic, he knew what the engine should sound like, and if it didn't sound just right, he could fix it himself. He found he enjoyed the challenge as well as the excitement of the race.

Soon, other Harley owners started winning races on their machines, which gave the young company a chance to boast that anyone could buy a Harley-Davidson right off the line and be a winner. In 1911, the founders told *Motorcycle Illustrated* magazine, "No, we don't believe in racing and we don't make a practice of it, but when Harley-Davidson owners win races with their own machines, hundreds of miles from the factory, we can't help crowing about it." These victories started coming fast and furious in the 1910s. In 1912, at a race in San Jose, California, the winner rode a Harley-Davidson to finish seventeen miles ahead of the second-place machine.

Because of his desire to be number one, Walter Davidson insisted on the highest quality standards in the motorcycles bearing his name. If he was going to be out racing, he wanted to be on the winning machine. Many of the other racers naturally envied him, because if he did find something wrong in the design of his bike, he could go back to his brothers at the factory, and they would make the necessary changes. It was like having a test pilot on your staff—only here the president of the company was out testing the product.

Chapter 7

A Family Affair

On September 17, 1907, the boys filed the necessary paperwork to incorporate, and the young Harley-Davidson Motor Company become a legal entity. And even though the United States was sunk in an economic depression and the stock market was in the dumps, all seventeen Harley-Davidson employees bought out the new company's stock.

The boys were no longer just boys, and the dream was now reality. Walter Davidson, my grandfather, was now thirty-one years old. He was the skilled mechanic and machinist who assembled the first motorcycle; as he was intrigued by the business end of things, he was now named company president. Bill Harley was a quiet man who loved to spend hours at his drafting table, and he took on the role of chief engineer and treasurer. Arthur Davidson, the pattern maker, became the secretary and general sales manager; he had the great gift of gab and loved to meet new people and travel, all of which made him an ideal salesman. And William A. Davidson, the eldest brother at thirty-seven, officially joined the firm. He felt most comfortable on the shop floor rubbing elbows with the other machinists and working the tools, so he left behind his job as the railroad toolroom foreman to become works manager for the new Harley-Davidson Motor Company.

The new titles were in name only, because they all worked side by side with their fellow employees, just like they had before incorporating. The only difference was now all three

Walter Davidson, 1910

Setting Up Dealership, 1907
After Harley-Davidson incorporated, Arthur set out to recruit dealers. Following the publicity trail of Walter's enduro win in New York State, Arthur began in New England and moved south and westward. Ten years later, he had signed up more than 800 dealers, with at least one in each of the forty-eight states. He then concentrated on building a dealership network around the globe.

Davidson brothers and Bill Harley were devoting all their time to making motorcycles.

Each one took on a role that he thought he would be good at and then went on to develop more specialized skills— whatever was needed to keep their business growing. Bill Harley continued his education, specializing in internal-combustion engines, and received an engineering degree from the University of Wisconsin at Madison.

The Davidsons were learning skills in other areas. Walter and William went to Chicago to learn all they could about oxygen-acetylene welding processes. Then my grandfather studied heat-treating techniques. After mastering these skills themselves, they taught them to their employees.

Arthur, meanwhile, concentrated his energy in learning the skills of merchandising and the value of advertising. It didn't take him long to convince his brothers and Bill Harley that advertising would give their company an advantage over the competition. They wanted to advertise, but as the demand for motorcycles increased, any extra money was spent on production. How could they justify slowing down production to advertise in order to have more demand? But Arthur was insistent. One of his new friends, Walter Dunlap, was a partner in the young advertising firm of Klau-Van Pietersom-Dunlap, Inc. Being a natural when it came to selling, Arthur sold his friend on the idea of publishing the first catalog for Harley-Davidson on credit. This was quite an accomplishment because this new Milwaukee advertising firm was itself just getting started and struggling for money. As a result of this act of faith, Harley-Davidson did all its advertising with Klau-Van Pietersom-Dunlap for the next fifty years.

As with many companies that had their beginnings in the late 1800s and early 1900s, the founders of Harley-Davidson virtually lived at their place of work. Work was their life. Families came second to their quest for success. If their children wanted to see them, they would have to go to where their fathers worked. My grandfather once said, "We worked every day, Sunday included, until at least ten o'clock at night. I remember it was an event when we quit work on Christmas night at eight o'clock to attend a family reunion."

The Harley-Davidson founders were not alone in this characteristic. The other early Milwaukee industrialists, such as the Pabsts, Gettelmans, Harnischfegers, Uihleins, Puelichers, Millers, Bradleys, and Brumders, set out with the goal of being successful, and all made work their passion. There was a common bond of respect and loyalty between these early industrialists. Later, as they became more successful and had time to relax, they relaxed together. And when times were difficult for any of them, they helped each other out.

All the employees—not just the founding fathers—worked many long hours. In 1907, the new factory had two doors set side by side, one for management and one for labor. My grandfather would tell us how everyone used to laugh at this, because both doors were used irrespective of what title you held. This helped build a family atmosphere at Harley-Davidson. When an employee needed a home, the Davidsons' father, my great-grandfather William C., supplied the lumber. All the employees would then pitch in and help with construction.

As the works manager, Bill Davidson spent most of his time on the shop floor. He was a quiet man who didn't want to be involved with the big decisions of running a business. He did have an office with a desk, but the story goes that this desk was used as a laboratory and was covered with hubs, shafts, bearings, and pistons that he was at work on. His door was always open to fellow employees who felt right at home sharing their joys as well as their troubles with him. This soon led to a feeling of trust and loyalty between Bill and his workers, and they affectionately started calling him "Old Bill." Liking this role, he gave baskets of food to his employees on the holidays, and if any of the employees needed to take some time off because of a sick family member, he knew he could count on Old Bill to understand. Bill kept a small black notebook in one of his many pockets into which he would enter the names of the employees that borrowed money from him— "just 'til payday," as they often promised. He seldom collected any of these debts from the long list of machinists, tool and die makers, welders, and assemblers until they came to him saying they had some extra money and would like to pay back the now-long-overdue loan.

Dealership, 1912
Proud Harley-Davidson owners pose in front of Henry McDaniels's motorcycle and bicycle shop at 111 State Street in Madison, Wisconsin. (State Historical Society of Wisconsin/WHI (X3) 41480)

As the company grew, many people called on Bill to sell him supplies, offer him prospective deals, or just to visit and chew the fat. Because he was so easy to talk to, they would stay too long for this busy man. What could he do to get them to leave in a polite way? His solution was to go out in the shop and bring in a big barrel that he placed in the corner of his office. He then filled the barrel up with peanuts, and when he felt he needed to get back to work, he would ask, "Do you like peanuts?" When they answered yes, Old Bill would reply, "Grab a handful on your way out."

My grandfather Walter took his new role of president seriously as well. He was driven by an inner desire to be the best at whatever he set out to do, whether it was racing motorcycles or run-

Comparing Modes of Transportation, 1912

An unknown Harley-Davidson rider and an auto driver examine each other's vehicle. (State Historical Society of Wisconsin/WHI (X3) 30863)

ning Harley-Davidson. If he was going to be the president, then he was going to be the best president he could be. Although he finished high school, he never had the chance to go to college, yet still he was a voracious reader and spent his spare time studying business skills. What he didn't learn in books, he learned by watching the other industrial leaders of the time. Being a perfectionist, he wasn't satisfied until his management skills grew, and he became known for his leadership qualities.

He knew how much quality had meant to him when he was racing, so he always insisted on the highest quality standards for Harley-Davidson motorcycles. Again and again, he would remind his co-workers, "Your real employer is the purchasing public, and there will be no acceptance of Harley-Davidson if we fail to give excellent service and full satisfaction."

Being a true Scot, he was frugal with every penny. He kept accurate records of all the expenses and would pore over them, looking for ways to save money and help the company grow. He lived a modest personal life, saving every penny he made to invest in the company's future.

In his dealings with employees, Walter was open and honest. Each employee, whether on the management or labor side, was respected for his contribution to the whole. The byproduct of this relationship was trust, which cannot be bought but only earned. My grandfather used to say time and again, "We pay a fair wage for a fair day's work."

In his relations with other companies and suppliers, Walter—and Harley-Davidson in turn—was famous for loyalty. Fred Winding and Henry Fuldner, two retired business owners who knew Walter through most of their lives, summed up their dealings with Harley-Davidson's president: "His word both in business and his personal life was as good as any contract that could have been drawn and signed. He was extremely loyal to the people who helped him get started." In addition to Klau-Van

Pietersom-Dunlap, the company's first advertising firm that worked on credit and became a trusted partner for fifty years, Walter remained faithful to one bank. The Marshall & Ilsley Bank of Milwaukee provided the young company with its first commercial loan after the Honey Uncle's generous family loan. Walter was so appreciative of this act of faith in his new company that he insisted on doing all the banking business with Marshall & Ilsley throughout the decades.

Part of the growing Harley-Davidson family were loyal dealers who sold the motorcycles. It was Arthur who first came to believe that the key to long-standing success would come only when there were dealers all over the country selling Harley-Davidson products. As early as 1910, he set out to accomplish this goal by building a nationwide dealer network. At first, no one thought a nationwide network was possible because the Harley-Davidson Motor Company's sole claim to fame was Walter's victory in the famous 1908 FAM Endurance Run in New York State. Arthur knew many people in the Northeast had followed that race, so that is where he concentrated his energy. With his gift of persuasion, it did not take long before he had a full roster of people signed on to be Harley-Davidson dealers.

Being the most outgoing of the brothers, Arthur was well suited to his job of selling. With his friendly personality and his gift for gab, no one was safe from his charm. If he had an idea that he thought was worth selling, watch out—he was unstoppable. His motto was "Our dealers must make money, and then so will we." With time, he traveled all over the world, setting up dealerships in Great Britain, Mexico, Canada, Australia, and New Zealand. In 1914, Dudley Perkins started a dealership in San Francisco that is now the oldest family-run Harley-Davidson dealership in the world.

Many a dealer would tell this story: "I would have a problem that I thought was huge and unsolvable. Arthur would come into my store and we would start talking. He would quietly listen, but after a short while, his eyes would start twinkling. Sure enough, as soon as I was through talking, he would tell me about another dealer somewhere else in the country that solved a similar problem. It didn't take long, and together we would solve my problem. Through the years, I always knew if I called Arthur for help, he would come, and together we would find a solution."

These dealers became trusted friends and would be loyal outlets for Harley-Davidson products through the years. They would remain dealers in both good and bad times because of the close, personal connection with Arthur Davidson.

Chapter 8

Turning Iron into Gold

Bill Harley and the Davidson brothers were unspoiled by their success. "The founding fathers want nobody to think they are wonders, and they disclaim anything but average capacity for mental and physical effort," reported the Milwaukee *Journal* newspaper in 1914. "You see them about the plant in blue flannel shirts. They meet their employees on an equal footing, remembering the days, not so far distant, when they themselves were 'at the bench.'"

Harley-Davidson had come a long way since the days when it took them a whole year to build three motorcycles in their shed. By 1914, the *Journal* stated that there were 1,570 employees at the factory, and 16,284 motorcycles were produced that year. One new motorcycle rolled out the door every five and a half minutes. It seemed that whatever Harley-Davidson decided to do turned into gold.

In 1907, the Milwaukee Police Department purchased a fleet of Harley-Davidson motorcycles as mounts for its patrols, giving more visibility to the young company. In 1915, the first motorcycles with sidecars were produced and were immediately sold to the postal service. It turned out the sidecar machines—affectionately known as "hacks"—were ideal for carrying the mail. In 1916, a unique monthly magazine named *The Enthusiast* was first published and sent out free to all Harley-Davidson owners. It is still being published today, marking it as America's longest continuously published motorcycle magazine.

In 1912, a promoter built what was known as a "motor-drome" in Milwaukee for motorcycle racing. Like the bicycle-racing velodromes from which they were derived, motordromes were circular racetracks built of rough pine boards and boasted high, banked corners; spectators sat in bleachers around the outside with the paddocks in the center of the track. At the new Milwaukee motordrome, Indian motorcycles could be heard roaring around the boards and taking home all of the racing victories—right there in Harley-Davidson's backyard!

Arthur Davidson in particular stood staunchly against motorcycle racing and waged a campaign in the pages of *The Harley-Davidson Dealer* warning all and sundry against competition. Arthur was keenly aware of the dangers of racing because many people he knew through the dealerships ended up victims on the track. Arthur was busy traveling all over the country working with the dealers and making new friends, and knowing Arthur's personality, I would say they did not sit around like gentleman: They probably shared a few shots and beers and swapped stories ripe with colorful language. When Arthur would hear of their deaths or of crippling injuries due to racing he personally felt the loss. He was especially incensed by the opening of the Milwaukee motordrome, and an editorial duly appeared in the *Dealer*:

Arthur Davidson's Motordrome Views

"Here is something we ought to warn our dealers against," said Sales Manager Arthur Davidson as he handed the publicity man a letter which he had been reading. It was from a Milwaukee automobile dealer who had been approached on a proposition of promoting a motordrome in the Cream City and was asking Mr. Davidson's advice.

"This is the time of year when the annual crop of

Harley-Davidson Endurance Team, 1912

With leadership from Walter (second from right), a team of endurance-run riders sit astride their Harley-Davidsons in the middle of Milwaukee's Wisconsin Avenue.

promoters and board track builders begin to sprout and it would be well at this time to drop a suggestion, to Harley-Davidson dealers especially, to leave the race track proposition alone," continued our sales manager and, there is probably no one in the motorcycle business who is better versed in the racing game and its seeming ability to produce publicity than Arthur Davidson.

"Any dealer who contemplates hooking up with a promoter in the 'murderdrome' business, I have found it to be my experience, has nothing to gain and everything to lose. Only the other day I was talking with a promoter and he was dilating on its wonderful possibilities as a money maker, saying that it practically was a gold mine. I could not help but recall what Mark Twain said about gold mines when he described a gold mine as 'a hole in the ground owned by a liar.'

"Any dealer who is approached on the board track business should remember what Mark Twain said about the gold mine. Of course the dealer should not take this to mean that we want him to go out and 'buck' that end of the racing game. We just want to suggest that they leave it alone.

"The board track game will work out its own destiny and in a mighty big hurry. I would hate to see one of our dealers get 'stung' on a bad venture. Better leave it alone in the first place. If somebody comes around and offers to 'let you in on the ground floor' don't jump at the 'opportunity.' It has been said there is a sucker born every minute. I guess the estimate must be true. It certainly is true that there is a lot of money dropped every minute on these 'ground floor' propositions.

"The lumber in a board track that has failed is not

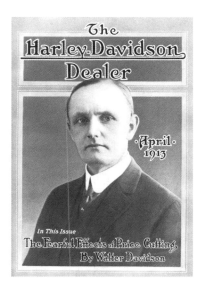

The Harley-Davidson Dealer, April 1913
Walter looks out from the cover of the factory's dealer magazine. Although only Bill Harley had formal education past his fifteenth year, each of the founders regularly wrote articles for the official magazines, including Arthur's vehement diatribes against racing.

worth a great deal. That has been the experience of the unfortunates who have taken a chance in dropping money into the motordrome game. There is nothing to the motordrome game any way that you look at it. Certainly it does not help the motorcycle industry. The killing of half a dozen riders every season and the occasional killing of a few spectators does motorcycling positive injury instead of benefit.

"Let the board tracks alone. The promoters are the only people who are getting anything out of the board tracks. But invite them to look elsewhere if they offer you 'a chance to get in on the ground floor.' There is no reason why you should chip in to help out a promoter who will drift on to some other town when the board track in your place has failed and the 'investors' are trying to figure how much of their money they can get back by selling the track for old lumber."

In another issue of *Dealer,* Arthur Davidson again railed against racing. His editorial entitled "How Many Lives Must Be Sacrificed To Speed," he stated:

The Harley-Davidson Motor Company has often been asked why it did not take part in the racing game. Our answer is: "We do not believe in it." And we have reasons for that answer.

Before going into those reasons, let us make the statement that the Harley-Davidson Motor Company can build just as good and as fast racing machines as any of the companies that are building them today. This is a broad statement, but we can prove it, because we did it previous to the time we dropped racing.

We can build freak racing machines, eight valves, auxiliary forks, lightened moving parts and everything "skinned" down to racing. But of what benefit would it be to us? We don't sell these freak racers.

They would not teach us anything in the way of design, because their design is altogether different than that of a road machine. They would be of no service, except possibly to amuse racing fans, make a little money for the promoters, and incidentally, secure a few records, which might be of use in selling our stock machines.

Perhaps you wonder why this was written. It was for no other purpose than to place emphasis on the stand we take regarding the racing game, its benefits and injuries to the motorcycle industry. A year ago we did not believe very much in the racing game, today we believe a

Lou Balenski, 1934
Lou was one of many who rode Harley-Davidson racers to victory. This 30.50 single was built at the insistence of Arthur Davidson: Long opposed to racing, he gave in to the other founders' desire to compete—as long as they built a racing single, which Arthur considered less dangerous since it wasn't as fast as the "killer" twins. (JHO Collection)

Lou Balinski
1934 Champ - Chi.,

ENTIRELY

$4,505,000.00 worth of Ha 1913 output of 17,000 mac and secured by deposits—

We can accept no more dealers until after October 1st.

We are exhibiting at the Chicago show, not to secure handle efficiently—but simply to give all an opportunity of experience in correct designing and honest workman.

This is the first time any motorcycle manufacturer ha actually turned away business the beginning of the year.

Our sales record—the selling in 12½ weeks of the entir that Harley-Davidson quality is supreme.

Harley-Davidson Motor (

PRODUCERS OF HIGH-GRADE M

"Entirely Sold Out," 1913
Sales were strong in the years prior to World War I, and Harley-Davidson's 1913 production run of 17,000 motorcycles was sold out in twelve and a half weeks, as noted in this ad from The Harley-Davidson Dealer.

great deal less, and we hope to see the time that it will be abolished completely.

But, no doubt, it will take more human sacrifices before the "speed craze" dies out. We are for the safe, sane rider, who uses his machine both for business and pleasure and enjoys his motorcycle as it was designed to be used.

Even though the company had vowed not to go racing, Indian's glories at the new Milwaukee motordrome was too much to take. Harley-Davidson refused to sit on the sidelines any longer, so it hired William Ottaway, a racing genius of the day. Ottaway designed Harley-Davidson's first racing motorcycle, and the company set forth to challenge Indian.

Bill Harley was big into racing, and in 1914, he established the company's first official Racing Department. Harley-Davidson's factory race team became known as the Wrecking Crew for their hard-won victories. Soon, the best racers wanted to be on the Harley-Davidson–sanctioned racing team, which was winning races everywhere in North America.

The move into racing was hard to swallow for some of the company founders—especially Arthur. The founders were split between those who loved competition and those who didn't like the thought of lending the Harley-Davidson name to a dangerous sport that was tied to speed and tragic deaths on the track. They had long, vehement discussions about how dangerous racing was. As a compromise to Arthur's distaste for racing, Bill Harley agreed to develop single-cylinder racers, which Arthur grudgingly saw as safer since they couldn't go as fast as what he called the "killer" big-twin racers.

In the early days of World War I, the booming British motorcycle industry stopped making motorcycles and shifted into all-

The Wrecking Crew, 1914
Embarassed by Indian's victories at the Milwaukee motordrome, Harley-Davidson hired Bill Ottaway to organize a racing team, which then attacked the nation's racetrack with a vengeance. The team soon earned the moniker "the Wrecking Crew." (JHO Collection)

out war-materiel production. Because of this, countries all over the world turned to the United States for the motorcycles that they needed, and Harley-Davidson got a good share of the business right from the start.

When the United States entered World War I in 1917, the U.S. Army took a cavalry mounted on Harley-Davidsons with them to Europe. In the next two years, the Army bought about 20,000 motorcycles for dispatch work and as scout vehicles.

The U.S. Army's use of motorcycles gave birth to another Harley-Davidson tradition, the Service School. In 1916, Mexican revolutionary hero Doroteo Arango "Pancho" Villa was angered by American support of the power-hungry and corrupt Mexican government, so Villa retaliated by sending raiding parties across the U.S.-Mexico border into Texas. President Woodrow Wilson would not stand for such impudence and sent the U.S. Army to save the day. But Villa and his band proved elusive, so American General John Joseph "Black Jack" Pershing stabled the horses his soldiers were riding in their vain effort to catch the revolutionaries and sent out a call for motorcycles.

On March 16, 1916, the U.S. War Department telegraphed Harley-Davidson requesting that a dozen motorcycles be shipped immediately to Fort Sam Houston, Texas, where they arrived two days later, ready for action. The motorcycles were equipped with armored Colt machine guns mounted on sidecars, as developed by William Harley. Pershing and his motorized cavalry chased Villa and his *banditos* away from Texas and into the deserts of northern Mexico.

This first use of the Harley-Davidson in the armed services taught the Army the value of motorcycles and motorized cavalry troops—and also opened the Army's eyes to the fact that it had no means of maintaining these new marvels. Once again, the company stepped in to save the day: The Army asked Walter Davidson to set up a school at the plant that would train military motorcycle mechanics. Thus began the Harley-Davidson

Service School, which has been turning out qualified mechanics ever since the first class graduated in 1917.

After the end of World War I, the Service School was expanded to provide education for dealers and their mechanics, passing on the hard-won expertise. Through the years, thousands of mechanics from all over the world have graduated from this school. So, Harley-Davidson owners have Pancho Villa to thank for the quality of motorcycle maintenance information that has been passed down through the decades.

When both the Mexican border conflict and World War I were over, there was additional demand for Harley-Davidson motorcycles from many of the servicemen who had ridden them or had been trained as mechanics and who now wanted a Harley-Davidson of their own. Even amidst the economic recession following World War I, the Davidson brothers and Bill Harley were busy trying to figure out how they could increase production to meet the new demand.

Not everything was a success at Harley-Davidson in these early years, however. At this same time, my grandfather and the other founders came up with the idea to expand their market to include bicycles.

The market for pedal bikes had boomed during the Gay Nineties and made millionaires of the bicycle builders. The first motorcycles were bicycles mounted with engines, such as the famous 1900 Thomas Auto-Bi from the E. R. Thomas Motor Company of Buffalo, New York, and the 1900 Orient from the Waltham Manufacturing Company of Waltham, Massachusetts. These two machines are credited as being the first production motorcycles in the United States. When the motorcycle became the next big thing, many bicycle manufacturers turned their hand to building motorcycles. George M. Hendee's Hendee Manufacturing Company of Springfield, Massachusetts, built bicycles before venturing to build its famed Indian "motocycle" in 1901 with the engineering know-how of Oscar Hedstrom. Colonel Albert Pope's Pope Manufacturing Company of Hartford, Connecticut, had built its fortunes on bicycles before entering the motorcycle marketplace in 1912 with its Pope V-twin. And Ignaz Schwinn of Chicago, Illinois, had also moved from bicycles to build the Excelsior motorcycle starting in 1911 and later purchased rights to the fabulous four-cylinder Henderson line in 1917. Harley-Davidson was doing things backwards.

Harley-Davidson launched its bicycle line in 1917, characterizing the non-motorized bike as a "true brother" to the touring motorcycle. The company's bicycles were subcontracted from a dedicated bicycle manufacturer, the Davis Sewing Machine Company of Watertown, New York. They were well made, attractively painted in the "soldier color" of olive drab green, and stylishly pinstriped in the same fashion and color as their larger, motor-driven siblings. Advertising of the pedal bicycles was primarily directed to pre-teen boys and girls. It all sounded good at headquarters. But there was a problem, and it was a big one.

When the Harley-Davidson dealers were asked to sell the bicycles, they simply didn't want to. They were already stretched to the limit just filling the overwhelming demand for motorcycles. My grandfather always used to say that the dealers responded to the factory almost like a chorus, saying, "Why would we want to sell bicycles when we don't even have enough time to fill all our orders for motorcycles? Plus, it is a different type of person who wants a bicycle. The customers who come into our store want what a motorcycle can give them—speed without the work of pedaling. They think of a bicycle as a step back in time. We went into this business to sell motorcycles and that is what we want to do."

And so the dealers pushed the bicycles into the corners of the showrooms, where they sat gathering dust.

Harley-Davidson continued to produce bicycles for seven more years but in the end William, Walter, Arthur, and Bill were forced to agree with their dealers. At a time when it seemed everything they touched turned to gold, it was hard for them to see something turn instead into scrap metal.

Happiness Is a Harley-Davidson
This woman was obviously enjoying her ride in the sidecar.

Country Roads

Harley-Davidson dealer and family friend Hap Jameson leads the way on a summer ride.

Chapter 9

Family Matters

Because my grandfather Walter took his role of being the president of their young company so seriously, he put off marrying until he was thirty-four years old. He always said he was too busy working to take on the responsibility of a wife and family. But now the company was doing a landslide business, and he thought the time was right to look for a bride.

Just a short motorcycle ride from the Harley-Davidson factory, at 14th West Vilet Street was a local watering hole and liquor store that my grandfather, his brothers, and their friend Bill Harley retired to for a drink when they wanted to relax. The German-immigrant owner, Adolph Rosenheim, admired these young Davidson and Harley founders for their industriousness and drive to succeed. He had two daughters: Emma, the eldest, was a feisty girl who with her younger sister, Clara, loved to laugh and enjoy life. Walter, being on the serious side, was attracted to Emma, and when he asked for Emma's hand in marriage, approval was given by all the German relatives. From my grandmother's point of view, stepping up from being a bar-owner's daughter to becoming the wife of Walter Davidson, president of the fastest-growing success story in Milwaukee, was a dream come true, and she was a real-life Cinderella.

In 1910, Emma and Walter were married and bought a home at 3223 West Highland Boulevard within walking distance of the factory. The other founding fathers and their families already were living nearby. Their wives became good friends, just as in the early 1900s the Davidson and Harley sons had become best buddies.

The Four Founders, 1910s
From left, William A., Walter, Arthur, and Bill Harley.

The wives had their own sense of humor. My father, Gordon McLay Davidson, was Walter's first child and Margaret was Arthur's first child. Because the babies looked so much alike, their mothers thought it would be great fun to switch buggies and then stroll over to the grandparents' house pretending they each had her own child. Watching the grandparents *ooh* and *aah* over the wrong child brought on fits of laughter from their mothers.

As the families grew, the cousins ran in and out of each other's houses depending on whose mother was baking the best sweets. There was never a reason for loneliness because they could always find a willing listener among the many relatives. If you were mad at your parents, you could always run next door and tell your grandparents how awful you thought your parents were. Sympathy was always close at hand. It was like the Scottish clans of earlier days when families stayed together to help each other in both good as well as bad times.

My grandmother Emma soon discovered she did not like spending all her time raising children. The other founders' wives seemed to thrive on it, but not my grandmother. What could she do? She knew it wouldn't do any good to ask her husband, Walter, to spend more time at home, because for him the factory was his life. She decided to hire a maid.

My grandmother found a fourteen-year-old girl named Kathryn Drmolka who had just come to America from Bohemia. It soon became apparent that Kathryn's special talent was being a trusted nanny to my father, Gordon, and his two younger brothers, Walter C. and Robert J., who was known as Bobby. Kathryn chose never to marry and devoted her entire life to the Davidson family. She became my father's and his brothers' trusted friend to whom they turned to for guidance. After the boys grew up and married, Kathryn became a source of strength for my grandmother. When my grandmother's health started to fail, Kathryn took care of her with the same loving devotion she showed to my father and his brothers.

Whenever I visited Kathryn, she would share stories of her life in the Davidson family. Her voice would fill with pride when she talked about "her boys." It did not matter that they were now grown up and had families of their own; they were still "her boys." One time she told me, "The years I spent raising your father and his brothers were the happiest times of my life. I came to America without anything and was happy to find a

Riding Side-Saddle No Longer, 1910s
Harley-Davidson ads promoted women riding motorcycles as early as the 1910s—which was fancy thinking for the day, to say the least. The women "models" used in the pictures were typically the founders' wives and children. (JHO Collection)

Fishing Trip, 1910s

William Davidson rides in the sidecar with Bill Harley at the controls after a successful fishing trip. This was the way the founders thought their motorcycles should be used.

nice family that wanted me to live with them and take care of their children. Those children became my children, and I felt like a mother to them."

Like a devoted mother, Kathryn saved everything the boys ever did, such as crayon drawings, and photographs of them growing up through the years. After my grandmother passed away, my father and his brothers took care of Kathryn. She was always included in all our family functions.

Like Kathryn, it seems there was always one woman in each of the branches of the Davidson family who chose not to marry, but instead dedicated her life to taking care of any relatives who needed help. Maggie Davidson devoted her life to her sister's husband and his children after her sister died. Janet, the founders' sister, devoted her life to taking care of her father, mother, and uncle. Another cousin, Margaret McFarlane, devoted her life to taking care of sick relatives.

If my father, his brothers, and his cousins wanted to see their fathers, they walked over to the Harley-Davidson factory. Because of this, they spent much of their young lives down at the factory playing along the railroad tracks.

My dad told me this story: "One time my brothers, cousins, and I were playing with some friends on the railroad tracks. We were having a great time hopping the freight trains that were coming in and out of the factory. We had just jumped on when my friend Jimmy Taylor lost his grip and fell under the wheels. It was a terrible sight and we were scared. His leg was cut off, and we knew we needed to get help immediately.

"As afraid as we were of what our fathers might do to us for our foolishness, we had no choice but to go to them for help. My father ran down, scooped Jimmy up in his arms and rushed him to the hospital.

My friend Jimmy lived, but his leg was replaced with a wooden one. None of us ever played on the railroad tracks again. Jimmy's wooden leg didn't slow him down, because if he got mad at you, he would kick you with this hard wooden peg. We did not know anyone else who had a wooden leg, so we thought Jimmy was pretty cool."

By 1920, Harley-Davidson was the largest motorcycle manufacturer in the world, both in factory floor space and in the number of machines produced annually. It was one of the largest advertisers in the United States, with a yearly budget of $250,000, a huge sum in those days. Harley-Davidson boasted dealers in sixty-seven countries around the globe. Plant tours were conducted on a daily basis, a practice that continues today.

Feeling secure in the fact that their company was successful, my grandfather, his brothers, and Bill Harley started to enjoy the rewards of all their efforts. They began to take time off to pursue other personal interests. The founders found relaxation on the lakes near Milwaukee. Each founder chose a different lake at which to enjoy his time away from work. Arthur Davidson and his family had a summer home at Lake Ripley. Bill Harley had a summer home on Beaver Lake. William Davidson went to Pine Lake, and my grandfather went to Pewaukee Lake. All their children grew up playing in and around the water, while their parents relaxed before heading back to the city, to the ever-increasing demand for motorcycles.

The founders' father, William C., was now in his seventies and, as in his younger days, preferred to spend much of his time alone. His favorite pastime was fishing in a small boat on Lake Ripley. It didn't seem to matter whether he did or didn't catch any fish; he just wanted to be out on the lake by himself. Who knows what he was thinking about? Maybe he was dreaming of his homeland of Scotland while drifting across the clear waters. I am sure he was thankful for his life in America and for the time he spent watching his sons become successful, as he was very proud of them.

But now there were all these grandchildren around, and he really did not have any patience with them. People that knew him called him a dour, taciturn Scotsman. His grandson, Arthur's son Arthur H., remembered one incidence: "When I was a small boy of about eight years old, I begged my grandfather to take me and my cousin William Marx out fishing. Finally agreeing, he rowed out into the center of the lake. It wasn't long before we started asking questions and were wriggling around. I could tell from his face he was getting upset, but he didn't say anything. I couldn't understand why he started rowing to the closest shore. Upon reaching that shore, he said just two words: 'Get Out.'

"That was the first and last time my grandfather ever took any of us grandchildren out fishing. We didn't understand why he didn't want us around. As far as we were concerned, he was a crabby old man."

The Davidson founders were proud of their Scottish heritage and taught their children many Scottish customs. Arthur Davidson taught his children, Margaret and Arthur H., the Highland fling and the sword dance. When they performed for my great-grandparents, it was said, "many a tear dropped while they remembered their Scottish homeland."

My grandfather, Walter, had two Scottish kilts brought over from Scotland for his children to wear whenever there was a parade or celebration. One time he called in a professional photographer to take their picture, which started a family tradition in which each generation had its picture taken in these kilts in remembrance of their heritage. When I was a young girl, my picture was taken with my sister in these same kilts, and when I had children, the tradition continued. Of course, my boys thought it was "dumb" putting on "skirts" and did not want the pictures displayed on our living-room wall.

Walter, William, and Arthur Davidson also joined the St. Andrews Society, a club for people who loved their Scottish heritage. One time, Arthur, with his storytelling ability, agreed to dress up in a kilt and do an impersonation of the famous Scot

Visiting Dealers, 1923

Bill Harley pilots the motorcycle with Walter in the sidecar seat as they visit Harley-Davidson dealers.

Scottish Heritage, 1918
Brothers Walter C., left, and Gordon photographed in Scottish kilts—the start of a Davidson family tradition.

singer, Sir Harry Lauder. It was only supposed to be for a small group of friends, so Arthur thought it would be great fun. Somehow, word spread that the "real" Sir Harry Lauder was coming all the way from Scotland to perform, and Scots from all over Wisconsin made a pilgrimage to the event.

When Arthur saw the crowd, he was in a quandary. Even if he went out on stage and announced the mistake, the people who had traveled a great distance would be angered. What should he do? Arthur was never known to run away from a challenge, so he started thinking: "Maybe I could pretend I am the real Sir Harry Lauder. I could go out on stage, tell a few stories, sing a few songs, and then quickly leave by the back door." He liked the excitement of pulling off a prank. He did just as he schemed, and no one ever found out that he was an impostor.

The founders liked playing jokes on one another as well. One time when they were hunting, Bill Harley fell asleep in his duck boat. He snored so loud that pretty soon ducks were swimming all around him. Arthur said to his friends, "Let's shoot some ducks and scare Bill at the same time.' So, they took another boat out, positioned themselves behind Bill's boat, and shot right over his head. Bill woke up, jumped straight up into the air in fear and then, seeing all the dead ducks around him, started laughing.

Another time when Bill Harley and Arthur were hunting, they were given a present of some special hickory-smoked bacon from Arthur's older brother, William, who was no small prankster himself. They were told it was to be saved for a special occasion. Arthur kept it in the icebox for months, waiting for a family gathering. Every time someone opened the door to the icebox, this wonderful aroma of hickory came from this package. It was hard to wait for a special occasion but finally such a time came. Everyone was waiting for Arthur to unwrap this delicacy. Inside the greasy paper wrap was a plain old piece of hickory wood. The joke was on him, and everyone, including Arthur, laughed.

Harley-Davidson Riders, circa 1918
(Bessie Davidson Collection)

With the ongoing success of their company, the founders made choices on where they wanted to live and how they wanted to spend their wealth. The Davidson founders each went in a different direction.

Like his father, William A. did not like to draw attention to himself, and he lived a quiet life in Milwaukee. Many people said he was the heart of Harley-Davidson because he always carried the burden of worrying about the employees and their families. "Old Bill" took on a paternal role at the factory.

During the summers, William A. vacationed on Pine Lake. Again like his father, he enjoyed the solitude of being alone out in a fishing boat. While his wife spent her time working in their large, beautiful flower gardens, he drifted across the lake. I was told that he never forgot he was the son of a Scot immigrant who came to this country with nothing but a willingness to work hard. He told his family and friends how thankful he was for all his blessings, and how he still had to pinch himself to be sure he wasn't dreaming about how successful he had become.

Arthur had spent his summers as a young man working on Cash Potter's farm in Cambridge, Wisconsin. Now he was grown up and had enough money to live anywhere he wanted. Remembering how much he had loved the country, he bought land in Waukesha County and moved his family onto a farm. Arthur had spent most of his life traveling the world setting up Harley-Davidson dealerships; now he could not think of any place he would rather be than on his farm.

Arthur believed in investing his time and money in youth. With his gift of persuasion, he promoted charity drives for the Boy Scouts, Boy's Club, and 4H. He started a new concept in fund raising by matching donated money with his own to build the Pilgrim Congregational Church on North 52nd Street in Milwaukee.

When my grandfather took on the role of being the president of their young company, he made it his passion to be the best in his field. It wasn't long before he became known for his astute business skills, and other business leaders in the area were asking him for his advice. He was named a director on the board of two prestigious businesses in Milwaukee: the First Wisconsin Bank—Wisconsin's largest bank—and the Milwaukee Gas & Light Company. He also became a trustee of the Northwestern Mutual Life Insurance Company. With all these accomplishments, he received a lot of attention, and just like when he was racing, he enjoyed it. He and his wife, Emma, started socializing with the other industrial leaders in Milwaukee, and soon they became known among the movers and shakers of Milwaukee. Some of their friends were the Harnischfegers, Pabsts, Evinrudes, Uihleins, Puelichers, Gettelmans and other business leaders of the city. Together they became a close-knit group who

Military Motorcycles, 1919

Harley-Davidson supplied some 20,000 motorcycles to the U.S. Army in World War I for dispatch work and as scout vehicles. After the end of hostilities, Walter (second from the left) led soldiers in a motorcycle parade in Germany. (Bruce Davidson Collection)

Post–World War I Optimisim, 1919

Following World War I, Walter toured Europe to promote Harley-Davidson. Here, he was taking an English officer for a spin.

The Four Founders, 1920s
Standing in front of the factory, from left, William A., Walter, Arthur, and William S. Harley.

not only worked together but also relaxed together. They had their own code of loyalty to one another.

Even though he was now considered a powerful Milwaukee industrialist, my grandfather was a real gentleman when it came to manners and integrity. He became incensed whenever an employee was treated disrespectfully. He sat on the board of directors for a handful of other companies. One day he was at a directors' meeting when the president of the company bawled out one of his custodians in front of my grandfather and the rest of the directors. When the president was finished, my grandfather stood up and said, "You were uncouth, rude, and a bear. I do not want to be on the board of this organization with people like you." He walked out and from that day on, he had nothing to do with this man. My grandfather told us, "There is nothing wrong with getting upset with an employee and letting him know, but it should always be done in private and not in front

The Founders' Wives, 1920
From left, Bill Harley's wife, Ann; Walter's wife, Emma; William A.'s wife, Mary; and Arthur's wife, Clara.

of his fellow employees."

My grandmother Emma became known as a trendsetter. In her early years she dreamed of having enough money to wear the latest styles, and now she could do it. She subscribed to the latest fashion magazines from New York and Europe, dressed accordingly, and was the center of attention at parties. Her goal was to be the first woman in Milwaukee doing whatever was the latest craze. I was told that she was considered risqué. Other women would watch to see what Emma would wear and do, and then follow her lead. She was one of the first women in Milwaukee to wear nail polish and go to a beauty salon.

It became important to my grandfather to show the world that the Davidsons had made it up the economic ladder. He hired a chauffeur named Rollie who would drive my grandmother wherever she wanted to go. Even the children could not escape this new lifestyle. My father remembered: "When I was a young boy, my parents made my brothers and me wear suits to school and be driven by the chauffeur. We were embarrassed and mad that no one bothered to ask us if we wanted to be different from our friends. Of course we didn't! We wanted to walk to school and dress like the other children in our neighborhood. My parents, like the other newly wealthy in Milwaukee, wanted to show the world that they were successful."

On the other hand, my grandfather couldn't bring himself to move away from the immediate neighborhood of the factory because he wanted to be close at hand both day and night. Instead of moving to one of the more fashionable neighborhoods, he lived on Highland Boulevard near the old factory until the late 1930s.

During the summers, relaxation time was spent at the stylish Lakeside Resort on Pewaukee Lake. Nanny Kathryn would always be with them to take care of the boys, so my grandparents could concentrate on entertaining. They and the other newly rich started to see who could have the most lavish parties. It was said that if you ever attended a Davidson party, you were bound to have had a good time. I think my grandfather worked so hard becoming a successful industrialist that he wanted to enjoy the fruits of his labor in a way that would bring him the most enjoyment. Like everything else he did in life, his parties had to be the best.

Around the mid 1920s, my grandfather decided he wanted to do something new. He felt he had accomplished his dream of being successful in business. Always a voracious reader, my grandfather loved books about foreign countries, but had been too busy running the factory to ever think about actually visiting them. But soon his sons and nephews would be working at the plant. With business being so good, he thought to himself, "Why not?" His wife was a willing partner, and together they set out to visit as many countries as possible. They traveled on the most luxurious liners of the day and collected fine antique fur-

The New Generation, 1921
Walter with his three sons, from left, my father, Gordon, Bobby, and Walter C.

niture to be shipped back to the United States

While on their travels, my grandmother started collecting unusual dolls from each country they visited, soon amassing a collection of more than two hundred original dolls. Each doll had its own stand and label that indicated the country the doll came from and how old the doll was. When they later built a new home on Lake Drive, these dolls were kept in lighted display cases next to my grandfather's racing trophies.

When I was a small child, I would turn the lights on in these display cabinets and immediately feel like I had stepped into a fairyland. But as you can imagine, these dolls were not for playing. I remember looking in these cases and feeling sorry for the dolls. I thought they looked lonely and wanted to be taken out and played with by some loving child. Maybe they even came alive and played together when no one was around.

I found a family book of memories written by my grandfather's sister, Bessie. In an entry about Walter, she wrote, "My brother, Walter, is energetic, capable, straightforward, always punctual, and a perfectionist. Like our father, you can set your clock by his punctuality. He is always on time and insists that each of the members of his family be on time."

From reading this and other personal accounts of his life, I can see why people said he was a strong-willed person who did things in his own way. Being energetic, capable, and straightforward are wonderful character traits that are usually easy to live with, but his demand for punctuality was hard on his children.

My grandfather's perfectionism was also tough for his children to handle. He always wanted to be the best at whatever he set out to do. Because of this character trait, he was not content with the company until it was making what he considered to be the best motorcycles on the market. He set high standards for the company—just as he would for himself—and expected everyone to adhere to them.

Walter Davidson, 1921
A signed portrait of Walter when he was forty-five years old. (State Historical Society of Wisconsin/WHI (X3) 52836)

Sailor Outfits, 1921
My grandmother Emma stands behind her boys: from left, Walter C., Bobby, and my father, Gordon.

My grandfather had three boys. My father, Gordon, was the oldest and tried to always do what his father wanted. My Uncle Bobby was the youngest and also followed the straight and narrow path that his father set out for him.

But there was one more son in this family, and his name was Walter C. He was named after his father and inherited his forceful personality. Like many middle children, he didn't like rules and time restraints.

My grandfather was used to giving orders that others followed, and this of course included his children. Walter told his son Bobby that he was to become an attorney so he could take care of legal matters for the company, and Bobby was duly sent off to the University of Wisconsin Law School. But his other son Walter C. did not want to follow the rules and live the life his father had set out for him. He couldn't find any school that he wanted to stay in. The more his father pressured him to do well in school, the less he tried. His goal was to prove to his father that he could do whatever he wanted.

Like many middle children, he rebelled and enjoyed life to the fullest. He had a wonderful, outgoing personality and made friends easily. Many people compared him with his Uncle Arthur, who had this same outgoing personality. Walter C. looked at all the founders, and decided that he liked his Uncle Arthur the best. He then convinced his dad that he would learn more by taking a job at the factory than trying any more colleges. He knew he was a good talker and had the right personality to be in sales, so one day he asked his father to give him one more chance by letting him follow his uncle Arthur around and learn all he could about selling motorcycles to the dealers. His father, who by this time was at his wits' end with this rebellious son, gave his approval. He was relieved that his son wanted to try something besides getting in trouble at school.

Walter C. traveled with his Uncle Arthur to dealers around the country and was a natural because of his friendly nature. He loved the excitement of being on the road. He always told us

Davidsons in the next generation, "I am glad I didn't do well in school. If I had, I might have ended up in an office without the chance to travel and meet so many nice people."

Like Arthur, Walter C. loved the countryside, and when he married, he bought a place in River Hills, Wisconsin, with enough land for his four children to enjoy. He played polo in his time away from the company, and his children all rode horses.

During the early years, the Davidson founders worked hard to make their company successful. At the same time, their mother, Margaret, was always quick to remind them of her belief, "You must always give back to your community for all your blessings." As the company became established, each founder selected the charities that interested him and supported them with large gifts of money and time. Besides their churches, some of these charities in Milwaukee included the Boy Scouts, Boys Club, the YMCA, Community Chest, Prospect Home for the Aged, 4H, and struggling young businesses. The youth of America was a matter of vital concern to Arthur Davidson, and being a great advocate of the outdoors, he bought some land ten miles from Milwaukee and gave it to the Boy Scouts, who named it Camp Arthur Davidson.

My grandfather Walter focused his attention on helping small businesses get a start. He never forgot how his Uncle James McLay gave him his first loan to build their first factory. He was so thankful to all the people who had helped Harley-Davidson get its start that he turned his attention to helping other young businesses get started.

Walter and His Son Gordon, 1920s

Family Traditions, 1927

Because the founders lived and breathed motorcycles, it was rare to get them all together for a family dinner. Their mother, Margaret McFarlane Davidson, (far right) is at the head of the table with the youngest of the founders' children, Jimmy Davidson, in the high chair.

A New Generation of Davidsons, 1923
Walter pilots a sidecar rig with his eldest son, Gordon McLay Davidson, in the sidecar. My father's middle name was in honor of the Honey Uncle, James McLay.

TT Racing, 1930s
TT, or Tourist Trophy, races were run on closed-circuit dirttracks with left- and righthand turns as well as the occasional jump. They were held in all weather.

Joe Ryan, 1920s

Joe was with Harley-Davidson almost right from the start. He was a big, gruff Irishman with a flair for colorful language, and he became manager of the Service School. He worked his whole life at the company and was loved by all—except perhaps the secretaries who would blush and hide when he lost his temper. (JHO Collection)

Harley-Davidson Dealership, 1921

Guy Webb's shop in Minneapolis, Minnesota, displayed several of the commercial models that Harley-Davidson marketed, including sidecars for delivery companies and a dry cleaner.

Hunting Sketch by Bill S. Harley, 1930

Along with fishing, the founders were avid hunters—and along with being a draftsman, Bill Harley was also quite an artist. This was his Christmas card from 1930.

Chapter 10

Do You Know Where Your Children Are?

In the summer of 1929 when my father was seventeen, he decided he needed some adventure in his life. He and his brother Walter C. and cousin Allan, who were both sixteen, were also ready to seek excitement. What could they do and where could they go? Their fathers considered work to be the most important thing in life, so what could they say that would get their father's approval and let them have some fun? They came up with a great scheme: They told their fathers they wanted to test ride the latest Harley-Davidson products by taking three motorcycles cross-country to California, Mexico, Canada, and back. All told, they would ride these motorcycles more than 13,000 miles.

My grandfather and his brother William talked it over and decided the boys would be the perfect salesmen to travel to all the dealers across the country, showing off the durability and dependability of the Harley-Davidson motorcycles.

The founders also likely saw the cross-country tour as a way to introduce dealers to the next generation of company management. The constant financial turmoil at arch-rival Indian prompted Harley-Davidson to respond through the years by displaying its own solid Scottish character and standing. The

The Three Musketeers, 1929
The boys photographed at the factory before taking off for their trip out West on Harley-Davidson 45s. From left, Walter C., Gordon, and Allan. My dad was the oldest, at seventeen, while the others were just sixteen.

1929 tour by the new generation of Harley and Davidson boys was a symbol of the stability of future Harley-Davidson management. The arrival of the boys at dealerships across the West represented a message that the faithful dealers heard loud and clear: Here was the future of Harley-Davidson in the flesh. Indian might be in trouble with an uncertain road in front of it, but the management of Harley-Davidson was in the good hands of the families whose names were on the gas tanks.

With these thoughts in mind, the founders gave their nod to the boys' plans.

My father, Walter, and cousin Allan were itching to get started: They were about to take off on a wild adventure to see the world. They couldn't wait to experience the thrill of sleeping outside under the stars—although I did hear they were afraid of bears and snakes.

The boys packed their bags and loaded up their machines, loaned to them by their fathers' factory. They were hungry to be out on the open road without any parents to tell them what to do. After saying their goodbyes, they twisted open the throttles and aimed their machines west.

Their fathers had agreed to let them go only if they promised to stop at the Harley-Davidson dealers across the country. This was OK with the boys because they needed a place to stop and clean up now and then. Whenever they came to a city with a dealer, they were greeted with awe and respect for their courage in undertaking such an adventure. Each dealer would invite them to stay with him so the boys could wash up and talk motorcycles. The boys always told the dealers they were proving the motorcycles were trustworthy for going long distances on the poorly constructed roads of the day. When asked if they were afraid of their motorcycles breaking down on the road, they laughed and said no because they were confident in their dads' ability to make the best motorcycles there were.

When they arrived in Seattle, Walter and Allan wanted to

Cross-Country Adventure, 1929

*While traveling to the West Coast, the boys stopped to visit every dealer on the
way. Here Gordon, Walter C., and Allan are lined up in front of Dudley
Perkins's venerable dealership in San Francisco. (Courtesy of the Harley-
Davidson Motor Company Archives; © 2001 Harley-Davidson; all rights
reserved)*

Joining Forces, 1929

Bill J. Harley and Bill H. Davidson join up with the other boys in Denver for the ride back to Milwaukee.

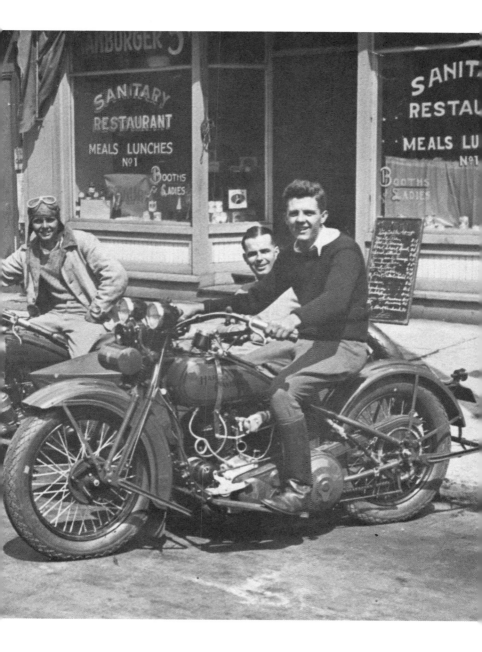

148

Warm Welcome, 1929

My father, his brother, and cousin Allan arrive in Denver after travelling 7,000 miles in 266 hours. They were met there by Bill H. Davidson and William J. Harley for the ride back to Milwaukee. Here they are in front of the capitol in Denver, Colorado, being greeted by officials. They were given a letter from the Governor of Colorado to deliver to the Governor of Wisconsin on their ride home. While in Denver they made their headquarters at C. A. Story's Harley-Davidson agency.

stop and relax, but my father wanted to keep going. He left them there, took off alone, and went up to meet the dealers in Everett, Washington, and Vancouver, British Columbia. The boys were quoted in *The Enthusiast* as saying, "Motorcycle riders are a fine set, ever ready to take off and hit the highways for happy miles behind the handle bars. They ride rain or shine, it makes no difference."

Each dealer tried to outdo the others in hospitality, taking the boys to the wildest and most exotic places. The dealer in New Mexico took them to Tijuana and showed them the works. In Los Angeles, the boys took a skyward ride in the famous Goodyear blimp. The dealer in Seattle took the boys on an airplane ride. My dad's comment in *The Enthusiast* was "Airplanes don't hold a candle to motorcycles for thrills and fun. Motorcycles are more fun because you are the one in charge."

Back in Milwaukee, Allan's brother Bill, who would become Willie G.'s father, decided he couldn't stand missing all the action; the stories coming back were just too exciting. Maybe he could team up with his best friend, Bill J. Harley, the founder's son, and ride out to meet his brother and cousins in Denver, and then they would be able to share some of the adventure. Bill J. Harley was staying in Kansas, so Bill Davidson decided to take a new 1930 74-inch model with a sidecar down to pick him up and head west to Denver. They too had promised their fathers they would stop at dealers along the way to show off the new 74 with sidecar.

When Bill and Bill J. Harley arrived at Pike's Peak in Colorado, they decided to try a hillclimb with their machine. Because the motorcycle with a sidecar was a relatively rare sight in the United States, no one had ever seen one in a race up a hill before. To the spectators, it was a strange sight to see one boy riding the cycle and another sitting in an attached sidecar. When it was over, they were pleased with their motorcycle's performance, and people gathered around asking them what it was like riding one of these new-fangled machines.

Leaving Pike's Peak behind, they rode to Denver to meet the others. It was a great reunion with lots of tales to tell. It seemed Allan had decided in California to add a sidecar onto his bike to see how the new model would handle with just one rider. So now there were five boys with four motorcycles, two of them mounted with sidecars.

They pointed their machines back east toward Wisconsin, stopping in Madison to deliver a letter to the Wisconsin governor from the Colorado governor. Then on to Milwaukee, where each boy reported to his dad that the machines they were making were worthy forms of transportation.

Can you imagine the thrills these young boys had going across the country on motorcycles in 1929? Most of the roads were dirt, and there were no highway patrols to call if you needed help. My father said it was one of the most exciting things he ever did.

And he also said that he, his brother, and cousins never did tell their parents *all* the adventures they experienced!

After their trip out west, the young Davidsons and Bill J. Harley thought they were invincible. In 1930, Bill Davidson and Bill J. Harley decided to go racing and entered the infamous Jack Pine Endurance Run. My Dad and his brother Walter thought they would also have a go at it. I can hear my dad telling his brother, "We just returned from traveling over 13,000 miles across country on a motorcycle, so how hard could an endurance race be?"

They would soon find out.

The Jack Pine enduro was a nationally known race organized at the time by the Lansing (Michigan) Motorcycle Club and run over hundreds of miles of northern Michigan wilderness. In 1930, the competition traversed 420 miles, and riders were awarded points that could tally up to a possible 1,000 if they reached checkpoints on time. The tour was nicknamed the "Cow Bell Classic," as the winner was awarded the Jack Pine Trophy, a cow bell inscribed with the victor's name.

Everything started out okay for my dad and his brother, but it wasn't long before they were in mud and rocks, slipping and falling with their bikes. They even went through the midst of a forest fire, gunning their stock Harley-Davidsons to hustle through the flames. Things were looking grim by the time they reached the middle of the course. Walter's hands became so tired his fingers locked in position, and he couldn't undo them. My dad and his brother both became so exhausted that their bikes fell over, and there they stayed in the mud, calling for their nanny, "Kathryn! Kathryn! Come and get your boys."

My dad remembered that race to the end of his days: "It was one thing, going with my brother and cousin on a fun trip without any time restraints. It was another thing to see how hardy I could be against other riders in a timed event." He definitely did not inherit the gift of racing from his father.

The 1930 Jack Pine may have been the event that rid my dad of any racing aspirations, but for his cousin Bill, it was an event that became part of family history.

While my dad and Walter were picking themselves out of the mud, Bill Davidson and Bill J. Harley were riding at the front of the pack. When they came to a checkpoint, Bill Davidson leaned over from his stock 45-inch motorcycle to Bill Harley and said, "You know, Bill, I think I stand a chance of winning this event but my watch is broken." Without a word and without a second thought of his own chance of winning, Bill Harley removed his own wristwatch and gave it to his friend.

Bill Davidson went on to win the Class A Solo event with a near-perfect score of 997 points. As he accepted the cow-bell trophy, Bill Davidson paid homage to Bill J. Harley, saying, "I could not have done it without my best friend's unselfish act of loyalty."

Through the years, the Davidson and Harley families shared many memories but this one was always recounted to the children down through the generations, telling of the act of friendship between two young men and the value of loyalty and sacrifice.

Loyalty, 1930
Illustration by Paul Smith of Bill J. Harley handing Bill H. Davidson his watch so he could continue and win the Jack Pine Endurance Race of 1930.

Chapter 11

The Next Generation: My Dad Joins the Company

My father, Gordon McLay Davidson, was the oldest son of Walter and Emma Davidson. He was an excellent scholar and never would have thought to rebel against his parents. Except for his one summer of adventure when he was seventeen, he worked at the company whenever he was not in school. His father wanted him to go to Wharton School of Finance at the University of Pennsylvania. Dad never would have thought to say no; he simply packed his bags and went off to college, following his father's wishes.

My dad's cousin, William H., being six years older, had already joined his father and was learning the business. The founders believed that their sons needed to learn everything about building motorcycles—starting at the bottom. When my dad graduated in 1932, he joined the company in the sales department as an accountant. My dad's father told him, "You will take orders and do whatever you are asked to do by your Uncle William, Uncle Arthur, Bill Harley, and myself."

And so my dad began his life with the company.

Gordon and Doris Davidson

My Mother and Me, 1937

Family, 1938
*My father, Gordon,
holding me while my
elder sister, Barbara,
cradles a doll.*

By 1936, there were six sons of the founders working under their fathers' scrutiny at the factory: Walter Davidson's sons Gordon and Walter C.; William Davidson's sons William Herbert and Allan; and Bill Harley's sons William J. and John. The only found er who did not have any children working at the factory was Arthur.

Arthur's son, Arthur Harley Davidson, was younger than the others, but like his cousins, all he ever heard about from childhood on was talk of Harley-Davidson motorcycles. He as sumed he would join the company when he graduated from Dartmouth. He had his father's gift of being outgoing and eas ily liked, so he thought he would be perfect for a job in sales. He reminded himself that it was his father who set up the world-wide dealership network for the company. Even his name was a tribute to his father's best friend and co-inventor, Bill Harley.

Thus it seemed only fitting that after young Arthur H. graduated from college, he approached his father and asked, "I have learned many languages that will help me when I travel to foreign countries to set up dealerships. I want to work with you down at the factory and get into sales."

He never expected his father to say no, but that is exactly what he did say.

Arthur Davidson told his namesake son in his own outspoken way that there were too many sons of the founders already working at the factory. Arthur Harley Davidson should look for a different job.

Talk about disappointment! My Uncle Arthur told me, "I was devastated. What would I do now? What about all my schooling? Had it all been in vain? Why didn't my father want me in the company?" When Arthur H. pressured his father for more answers, all his father would say was, "There are too many cooks in the kitchen already."

Eventually, Arthur H. realized his father meant what he said, and he looked for other opportunities. He soon was working at Wacho Manufacturing, a rustproofing firm, in Milwaukee. He then co-founded and was chairman of the successful firm of Wenthe-Davidson Engineering, a fabricating shop that did work for Harley-Davidson during World War II, among many other clients. His career is a perfect example of the saying, "When one door closes another one opens."

In 1934, my dad married his high-school sweetheart. All through high school and college he went out with a beautiful, shy girl named Doris Burdick. All she ever thought about was this young, blond Davidson who grew up down the block from her family and zipped around with his brothers on motorcycles. Growing up with few material possessions, my mother said it felt like she was marrying Prince Charming. In later years, she would constantly tell me, "I not only married Gordon, I married his family and the Harley-Davidson dream." Whenever I heard my mom talk about my dad, she would refer to him as the first and only love of her life.

My Dad, the Model, 1934
Gordon models a leather jacket for a Harley-Davidson accessories catalog.

My dad and mom wanted to start a family immediately, and my sister Barbara was born on July 10, 1935. I arrived shortly after, on September 3, 1937. We were the first grandchildren for Walter Davidson, and he doted on us and spoiled us.

My mom and dad were enjoying the life they had always dreamed about. Dad was learning all he could from his father and uncles, while my mother was raising my sister and me and doing charity work. My mom called it the Fairy Tale Years, because they were so happy.

I was not the ideal child. My mother used to compare me with my grandfather Walter because I inherited his strong personality and was independent to a fault. If someone wanted to hold my hand, I refused. My mother recalled that I would argue over everything: If she said the sky was blue, I would say it was gray. I must have been a trying youngster. My mom used to repeat the childhood rhyme to me, "There was a little girl who had a little curl right in the middle of her forehead. When she

Checking Out the Competition, 1941
My dad (right) examines a Triumph twin at the Daytona Beach Races.

was good she was very, very good; but when she was bad, she was horrid." I hope I was never horrid, but I do remember my mother shaking her head in despair and saying, "I don't know what to do with you."

Work was very important to my dad. He was at the factory every day, including Saturdays, and if he missed a day, he would call to be sure everything was running smoothly.

He liked to dress in casual, comfortable clothes. He spent most of his days down on the shop floor so he saw no reason to wear a suit. He liked feeling he was one of the boys and did not have any airs of superiority. I remember my mother and his mother wanting him to dress up and buy the latest styles. He would say, "Why should I? My coat's not worn out; it's just getting comfortable. If it gets a hole in it, I would rather have it mended than buy a new one." He became attached to certain clothes. When he did need to wear a tie, it would most likely be a Scottish tartan. At Pewaukee Lake, he always wore an old green sweatshirt and a captain's cap. He definitely did not inherit from his father or his mother the desire to dress in the latest styles.

Dad drove a Harley-Davidson motorcycle to and from work, and when he did need to take a car, he would only drive a Chevrolet rather than the Cadillac that his mother thought was appropriate.

My father was much like his Uncle William and did not want to draw attention to himself or his family. He impressed on us that we were kids just like all the other neighborhood kids. He used to say, "You will grow up and live in a world made up of lots of different people, so you might as well learn from little on how to get along with everyone." Maybe he remembered back to how he felt when he and his brothers had to dress in suits and have the chauffeur drive them to school. Because of this belief, he sent us to the public schools, and we walked or took the bus where we wanted to go.

Like his father, my dad wanted to live relatively close to the factory, so when he decided to build a house he picked a lot in the western outskirts of Milwaukee in a suburb called Wauwatosa. He was only three miles from the factory so, if he had to, he could walk to work. My aunt and uncle on my father's side lived one block away in one direction and my aunt and uncle on my mother's side lived one block away in the other. My father's cousin lived next door.

Every year Dad packed up and went to the motorcycle races at Daytona Beach, Florida. He felt right at home hanging out with the racers and sharing their world. Back home, he told us many racing stories around the dinner table and as bedside tales; I would hang on every word, and it made me yearn to go along with him. He would patiently tell me that soon the racers would be coming to Milwaukee for the State Fair Races, and I could go to those. For me, it was as difficult to wait for those races as it was to wait for Christmas morning.

In the Paddock, 1941
*My dad (with sunglasses in the background) watches
as mechanics tune rider Babe Tancrede's Harley-
Davidson prior to the Daytona Beach Race.*

My mom and dad loved to throw parties. My father, like his parents, liked to have celebrations, but was not interested in impressing anyone. These were good years, and they worked hard and partied hard.

They partied with their friends from school, moving the parties from house to house. I would hear all the noise and wonder what was happening, but I was never allowed down in the basement during these parties. As a small child, I would sneak part way down the steps to watch.

Our house was the favorite party house because we had rooms set up to party in. There was always a lot of laughter and drinking. In our basement was a wine cellar filled with bottles of liquor. None of them had labels on so I often wondered if they knew what they were drinking. Another room had girlie calendars on the walls and gambling tables. I remember spinning the roulette wheel and watching the little ivory ball drop into the numbered slots. I always wondered why people thought this was a fun thing to do.

My friends always wanted to go down into these rooms when they came over to play. I couldn't understand why because they were rooms I had grown up with and didn't think they were special. Maybe I thought everyone had rooms like these in their houses, although I had never seen any.

I think these parties were the way these dedicated people released their frustrations. Were they making up for the years of Prohibition or the Great Depression? Or had my father and his brothers seen the parties that their parents threw and wanted to have a good time as well? Either way, they definitely did know how to have a good time.

Some of the best times I had with my dad were when he would take me with him to the factory. We would climb onto his motorcycle or jump into the car, drive down to the company's garage, and be greeted by Charlie. In my eyes, Charlie ran the garage and everything to do with it; I saw him as a very important man. He would greet us with a smile and a joke. If we had the car, we would leave it with Charlie while we were inside. Charlie would fill it with gas, wash it, repair anything that needed fixing, and have it ready when we were to go home.

Our next stop would be the switchboard, where Stella Forge worked. I called her "Stella by Starlight," and she called me "Jeannie Beannie" because I was built like a string bean. Stella lived in a flat on 35th Street and walked to work every day. She never married; rumor had it that she was married to the Harley-Davidson family.

Stella knew everyone's business at the company because she took care of everyone's calls. I would stand for a long time and watch as the switchboard lit up and she connected callers. My dad, his brother, and cousins said that Stella knew more of what was going on at Harley-Davidson than they did. If anyone wanted to reach one of them at any time of the day, she knew exactly where they were. They used to joke, "No one is safe from Stella."

Stella controlled the fate of anyone coming in the front door. If Stella did not like you, you were doomed for getting an order. You never got past her switchboard because she also controlled the doors. Most of the salesmen knew this and thus were especially nice to her.

I had total freedom within the company. My dad spent a lot of time down on the shop floor and knew everyone's name. He loved to tell and hear jokes, so when people saw him coming, they told him the latest ones. I never could understand them and didn't think to ask what they meant; I just knew that everyone liked my dad, and they treated me great.

I used to love spending my time down on the assembly floor. The men would set me on the line as the parts came through, and I would ride along. No one ever said, "Look out!" or "You shouldn't be down there by yourself." I always felt perfectly safe because all the men thought of me as their little girl.

I remember one time there was a strike going on, and some

Daytona Beach, 1941

of the workers were carrying signs and were shouting. They were
not letting anyone into the factory. I was scared until the guys
saw Dad and me. Then they wanted to tell him some new joke
that they were saving for him. After they talked and laughed,
they let us through the line into the factory.

Many times I would answer the doorbell and find presents for
my father from people who either wanted to thank him or
wanted favors in the future. My father often said, "The wealthi-
est man in town is Abe the scrap dealer." Abe would always leave
a case of the finest Scotch whiskey on our front doorstep. He
dropped it off, rang the bell, and then drove off. He entertained
my family by taking them to the finest restaurants in town.

One time I came down the stairs, and there were two three-
foot-long alligators looking up at me. These had been shipped
to us children courtesy of Billy Temple, the dealer in Miami
Beach, Florida. He thought my Dad would get a kick out of them.
I remember my Dad shaking his head and saying, "What the
hell am I going to do with two alligators?" He made some telephone calls, and we took them to their new home at the Mil-

waukee Zoo. For years thereafter whenever I would go to the zoo, I would always try to pick out which were "my" alligators. Many times there were lobsters kept in our garage, gifts from other dealers. I would open the door and there would be bushel baskets with lobsters crawling around. I wanted to let them all go, thinking they could survive in Pewaukee Lake. I don't know what my parents did with the lobsters, because I made such a fuss about killing them that we never had them for dinner. They probably gave them to their friends, who then dined in style.

Ever since I was a child, motorcycle racing had a special place in my heart. I had heard my father's stories of the racers, and I looked forward to going to the motorcycle races at the Wisconsin State Fair Park each year. To me, the sound of revving engines was pure exhilaration. My mother and sister did not like the dirt and the noise, but I couldn't get enough of it.

All the racers I met were lean, strong, graceful, and wiry. I thought they were brave and had excellent coordination and balance. They all wore safety helmets, steel-tipped boots, and colored leather suits to compete in championship races organized by the American Motorcycle Association. I would cheer when they roared into a curve, bumping their elbows. In the corners, sparks would fly from their steel-tipped boots as they extended one foot for control. For me, it was all pure excitement.

My dad knew all the racers, so he would take me into the pits while he talked and joked with them. Naturally I wondered why there weren't any tomboys in the world of motorcycle racing. To me, this was just another example of how girls never had as much fun as boys.

One time I came home to find one of my favorite racers sitting on our porch, none other than the famous "Smokey" Joe Leonard. He had just been named the first national champion under the new points system for the American Motorcycle Association–sanctioned races for 1954.

Smokey Joe was so very handsome compared to the teenage boys I was used to hanging around with. He sat with Dad on the porch and told stories about racing and how tough it was on his body: It took lots of stamina to keep in top form, and injuries just went with the job. He told me that racing wasn't all that glamorous when he got hurt and was in pain. He talked about how much he loved the thrill of competition; once he got out on the track, all he could think about was winning. As a teenage girl out there on the porch, I could have listened for hours to his racing adventures. I just thought he was the bravest man I knew.

Through the years, many of the champion racers came to our home. Brad Andres, who won the national championship in 1954, would stop by. Carroll Resweber, who dominated from 1958 to 1961 with his four consecutive national championships, was often a visitor as he was born in nearby Cedarburg, Wisconsin. Still, Smokey Joe was always my favorite, and I was thrilled when he came back to win the national championship in 1956 and 1957.

These men were usually rough around the edges, which made them all the more exciting to a young teenage girl. My dad would listen to the stories of life in the racing world, and I would sit there entranced by their tales. I was always in awe of their light-hearted manner when it came to the dangers of racing and the injuries they sustained in the course of a year.

Naturally I dreamed of racing, but in those days a girl would not have been allowed on the racetrack except to kiss the winner and hand him his trophy. The kissing was fine by me, but it was the racing that I wished for.

Every year our family packed up to go to Florida at spring break. We loaded in the car and started driving, stopping at the Harley-Davidson dealers in each city along the way. They would want to entertain my dad but would have to put up with all of us coming along. I remember they were trying to talk business while my sister and I were usually arguing over something silly like whose turn it was next to sit by the window in the front seat so she could stick her arm out and get a head start on a tan. In retrospect, with my influence it's a wonder Harley-Davidson ever made motorcycles.

On the way down South, we always stopped at all the fireworks stands, and my father would load up the trunk.

When we were in Florida, we would drive down to visit Miami Beach dealer Billy Temple, who always took us out on his fishing boat. Billy was the one who had shipped us the two alligators that ended up in the zoo. One time when we were a long way from shore with Billy, the boat sprang a leak, and water was coming up over the flooring. My mom of course was terrified for us children, but the men seemed not to be worried. We did make it back to shore but my mom never wanted to go out fishing with that dealer again.

There were many family traditions, and they were all controlled by my grandfather. All holidays were to be spent at his house. There were no exceptions, no excuses were accepted, and it never occurred to any of us to say, "I don't want to go," or "I want to go to my other grandparents." All the relatives were at the Davidson's. They always invited the family members of their sons' wives as well, so I don't think anyone minded that all the parties were held at the Davidson's.

Christmas was a special time. Each year we would make out our gift list. My parents loved Christmas, and our living room would look like a toy store when we came down the steps on Christmas morning. They would never put any presents out until we had gone to bed, so they must have worked all night wrapping gifts and filling the large living room.

There would always be one large present that no one expected. One year, three canoes were in the living room. One year, there were three tents. But the present I wanted the most would never be there. I would moan and groan and be a crabby child.

Stella by Starlight, 1940s

Stella Forge and my dad cut a rug. Stella knew everything that went down at the factory and became a close friend to our family.

Christmas afternoon always included a trip to Grandma and Grandpa Davidson's home on Lake Drive. I remember the decorations were golden and elaborate. There were servants everywhere and lots of food.

As children, we ran around and laughed and played. We thought we were very naughty when we would sneak into the servants' quarters to see how they lived. What did we think we would find? I don't know, but we were always disappointed when we discovered that their rooms looked just like our own bedrooms and bathrooms. It was all so strange to have a section of a home just for servants. But we were young, and maybe what enticed us was the excitement of breaking the rules. Yes, there was a rule that no one was allowed to go into the servants' area. Of course when we did go, if anyone was there, they were always nice to us and asked us if we wanted to look around and see their things. I felt like a child going into a haunted house. I knew I was not supposed to be there, but my curiosity was overwhelming. I half expected someone to jump out at me and start yelling. But of course they never did.

At night we opened presents, and I was always surprised when there, under the tree, was the one present that I had first and foremost on my list. One year it was a special yellow bicycle that I had wanted. My grandparents and my parents acted surprised, and I never did seem to catch on that the whole thing was planned.

On January 29, 1947, there was a monstrous snowstorm that crippled the city of Milwaukee. All traffic was stopped, and people were stranded in streetcars, buses, and in the factories. People who needed to get to a hospital were taken by toboggan. Being only ten years old, I thought the blizzard was absolutely great! There was no school, only playtime in a winter wonderland.

But for my Dad it was another story. I remember him pacing the floor at home worrying about the company. Finally he decided he had had enough worrying and strapped on my sister's skies. I begged him to take me along, and he said, "Sure, if you can keep up with me."

I ran to retrieve my skies as well and away we went, skiing right down the middle of the street in the midst of the snowstorm to get to the factory. When we got there, we went inside, and my dad walked all around just to be sure everything was all right. Sure enough, everything was just fine.

Then he said, "OK, let's ski home." We turned around and headed back into the face of the blizzard. It was just the kind of adventure I loved.

Doublewide Sidecar, 1930
This prototype sidecar sat two in style. (State Historical Society of Wisconsin/ WHI (X3) 34953 CF 508)

Chapter 12

The Motorcycle That Saved Harley-Davidson

The Great Depression that began with the crash of the stock market on Black Tuesday, October 29, 1929, did not affect Harley-Davidson right away because the movers and shakers of Milwaukee helped each other by giving one another work. This could not last, however. By 1930, Harley-Davidson's motorcycle sales were down and would continue to slide through the Depression years.

The one bright spot in those lean years was a young racer named Joe Petrali. He was a quiet, sometimes solemn man, but on the track he was another person. In races, he rode his Harley-Davidson as if his life depended on it, and he would not give an inch. After each checkered flag fell, Joe would report back to William S. Harley and his engineers on what technically worked and what did not. Joe Petrali's input was invaluable to the new designs of Harley-Davidson.

Even Joe's wins couldn't keep Harley-Davidson out of trouble during the Great Depression, however. Industry-wide, total motorcycle production plummeted from almost 32,000 cycles annually during prosperous times to a low of just over 6,000 machines by 1933—more than an 80-percent drop in just a few years' time. Harley-Davidson built just 3,700 motorcycles

Knuth's Klimbers, 1930s

Milwaukee dealer Bill Knuth sponsored his own race team, the Knutch Klimbers, and challenged all comers at hillclimb events. Hillclimbing became popular in the 1930s—especially at Harley-Davidson, as it was less dangerous than other forms of racing. Knuth worked closely with Bill S. Harley and others at the factory in designing race machines; they used to sit around the kitchen table and go over ideas together.

in 1933, and the company was hurting. My grandfather had to go out and pound the streets looking for subcontract work. Meanwhile, Harley-Davidson's arch-rival, Indian, was reduced to making coaster wagons.

One of Harley Davidson's field sales representatives named Alfred Rich Child had another idea. Child was the company's exclusive sales agent for Japan, China, Korea, and Manchuria. At the dawn of the 1930s, he negotiated a contract with Japanese businessman Genijiro Fukui that turned over blueprints for the current Harley-Davidson Model VL side-valve to the Japanese Sankyo consortium for the next five years. Precision machinery and tools and dies were also sold to the Japanese; they were not needed at Harley-Davidson at the time because of the lack of orders. The Japanese consortium began production of

**Knucklehead,
1935**
*The founders examine
one of the revolution-
ary 61 OHV
Knuckleheads.*

their version of the Harley-Davidson Big Twin bearing the name "Rikuo" on the gas tanks.

My grandfather hated to make this outright sale of licensing rights, but he could think of no other way out of the crunch the company was in. For years, he grumbled over what he believed to be a real steal by the Japanese. The founders consoled each other in the fact that they would have lost the Japanese market anyway due to the unfavorable yen-to-dollar exchange rate. It has been said that the sales of these blueprints and machinery were what eventually turned the Japanese nation on to motorcycles.

The sale of the Japanese license to build the Rikuo provided more than just a Band-Aid for Harley-Davidson's ills, however. With the money received from the Japanese, the drafting boards were dusted off, and plans were drawn for a new model that would ensure the salvation and the future of Harley-Davidson and be loved the world over. This new motorcycle was to be known among aficionados as the "Knucklehead."

The story of the development of the Knucklehead dates back to 1928, when a Harley-Davidson dealer by the name of Bill Knuth collaborated with the factory in building an overhead-valve 45 hillclimber.

The Knuth brothers ran the Harley-Davidson dealership on the company's home turf in Milwaukee County. All of the Harley-Davidson dealers were a chosen group and protected by the factory. If you were lucky enough to be a Harley-Davidson dealer, you were given special treatment; Harley-Davidson called the shots as far as what you could sell, and the company protected you by not letting anyone else in the area have a franchise. But people say Bill Knuth was a favorite of the company. Being right in the home city of Harley-Davidson gave the Knuth brothers a tremendous advantage over others. The founders were their good friends, and many a night was spent talking over new ideas.

Bill Knuth was a racing advocate. He loved hillclimb races, and professional riders ruled this event. The factory or a dealer provided a hillclimb bike, mechanic, and travel expenses. If the rider kept winning, he had everything provided for him. There were not as many injuries as on the flat tracks, so the founding fathers supported this sport wholeheartedly.

In 1928, the factory and Bill Knuth teamed up to build an overhead-valve 45 to contest the hillclimb races. According to Arthur H. Davidson, the factory worked hand in hand with Knuth in constructing this experimental and largely forgotten 45 OHV hillclimber, and it later inspired the greatest Harley-Davidson motorcycle of them all, the Knucklehead.

In 1930, Bill Knuth built a second 45 OHV hillclimber that was known as the "Knuth Special." In his book *Harley-Davidson 1930–1941: Revolutionary Motorcycles & Those Who Rode Them*, historian Herb Wagner quoted Chuck Wesholski, who has studied these 45 OHV motors. Wesholski commented that "the Knuth Specials were real special, reflecting insider factory connections and a very intelligent and imaginative mechanical mind."

Bill Knuth's work with Harley-Davidson was the starting point for Bill Harley in designing the 61 OHV Knucklehead. Bill Harley first began planning the 61 OHV as early as 1931, although it would be 1935 before the new model was introduced to the dealers.

While it was seen as a new motorcycle, the Knucklehead wasn't really new at all. By using the one-off 45 OHV hillclimb engines as the basis for the 61 OHV, Bill Harley maintained the lineage of his original 1903 motor. There was no break with the past; the Knucklehead was a development, a modernization of the faithful Harley-Davidson engine rather than a completely new beast. The "Knucklehead" moniker came from the lumpy rocker covers perched atop the engine; these rocker covers looked like the knuckles of a hand closed in a fist.

When the founders unveiled the new 61 OHV at the Harley-Davidson dealer meeting at Milwaukee's Schroeder Hotel, the

old-time dealers just smiled. They knew in their hearts that the king of motorcycles had been reborn. Harley-Davidson's V-twin engine had come around again.

The dealers were thrilled by the 61 OHV. At the dealers' banquet after the unveiling of the new Knucklehead, founders and dealers alike celebrated. One dealer, "Cactus" Bill Kennedy from Phoenix, Arizona, was so enraptured that he pulled a revolver in the middle of the dining hall and began shooting his six-gun at the crystal chandelier and hollering "Yip-eee!"

It was a day that would go down in Harley-Davidson history. The Knucklehead became the turning point in the company's battle to win back motorcycle sales during the Great Depression. With its overhead valves, it was a modern engine design for the American motorcycle market. The Knucklehead ensured the salvation of the company and became the foundation for the Harley-Davidson motorcycles that are still being built today.

Milwaukee's Finest, 1930
Milwaukee's police naturally rode on Milwaukee motorcycles.

"Fun All The Way"
Harley-Davidson's Knucklehead put the fun back in the motorcycle business for the company and dealers alike.

Harley-Davidson Faithful
With renewed faith thanks to the debut of the Knucklehead, happy Harley riders in formation at Daytona Beach in the 1950s.

Bathing Beauties, 1923
Harley-Davidson advertising was gradually getting racier, as these beachside photographs show.

Chapter 13

Harley-Davidson Goes to War

In 1939, war was declared in Europe, and it soon became a truly global affair, drawing in all nations around the world. President Franklin Delano Roosevelt warned the United States to prepare itself: It was becoming apparent that America could not stay out of war. On December 7, 1941, the Japanese forces of Emperor Hirohito attacked Pearl Harbor, and the United States went to war.

As in World War I, Harley-Davidson played a vital role by providing transport for Allied troops. In the fall of 1939, the first order for 5,000 motorcycles came from Great Britain because the West Midlands of England, where most of the world's motorcycles were produced, had been heavily bombed and manufacturing hampered. This was followed by orders from the Canadian and American armed services, resulting in the creation of the famed WLC and WLA military models. During the five years of Harley-Davidson's wartime production, some 90,000 motorcycles were produced for communication, scouting, and military police duties. The Soviet Army used two-thirds of this number in its push from the east toward Berlin.

Harley-Davidsons became known as the "soldier's friend," and thousands of soldiers were taught to ride, maintain, and love motorcycles. This enhanced Harley-Davidson's reputation and secured a lasting affection with the soldiers who were assigned to ride one. And, as happened at the end of World War I, the soldiers brought their new passion home. Because every country in the conflict was touched by the Harley-Davidson motorcycle, an interest and loyalty was created that strengthened the company's international recognition once the war was over.

Beyond the company's steadfast patriotism, Harley-Davidson was also known for its unswerving integrity. During the World War II years, when Harley-Davidson was making parts for the U.S. Army, Walter Davidson noticed there was a huge surplus, and the government did not need that large of an order. He contacted the government agent and told him to reduce his order, stating that the government was wasting its money. He was shocked and upset when the government agent told him not to be bothered—that was just the way the government did business.

Being an astute businessman, my grandfather was ashamed of this practice, knowing that no business could be run so poorly. He sent his brother Arthur to Washington, D.C. to dissuade the Army procurement office from buying and stockpiling spare parts that would never be used. But Arthur's trip was also in vain: The procurement officer informed him he'd lose his job if any of the parts on his list were missing.

In the end, Harley-Davidson was forced to send them the excess parts, and just as my grandfather expected, they were never used.

Chapter 14

Grandfather Dictates the Future from His Hospital Bed

My grandfather did not live to see the end of World War II. In February 1942, at the age of sixty-six, my grandfather was sick and knew he was dying. He did not want to let anyone see him die—including his wife and family members. In the hospital, he ordered a nurse to stand at his door and keep everyone out except the doctor.

His nephew Arthur H. Davidson remembered an incident at the hospital: "I was in the same hospital having minor surgery and didn't know of Uncle Walter's edict about having visitors. Knowing how much Uncle Walter liked to read, I took him a book and walked right into his room. Uncle Walter acted surprised, thanked me, said goodbye, and then sternly warned me, 'Don't ever come back!'"

Right before he died, my grandfather called his sons and nephews into his hospital room. He had made up his mind about who would take his place as the president of Harley-Davidson. His oldest son, my father, Gordon, was just thirty-one years old

Walter Davidson at His Desk, 1940

**One Founder Left
to Guide the
Company, 1947**
*Arthur (right) stands
beside my dad and
other managers and
workers to celebrate
the 10,000th lightweight machine built.
This M-125 was the
first new model
introduced after
World War II, and
10,000 of them were
sold in the first seven
months of 1947.*

189

and was a quiet, hard worker. His nephew, William H., was thirty-seven and seemed to pattern himself after his Uncle Walter. My grandfather looked at the young men standing at his bedside and announced that William H. would take over his role of president. My father would be the vice president of manufacturing.

I have often wondered what kind of person could have that much control over his wife and grown children that they would not walk right past the nurse and insist on entering his room. I can't imagine any family member staying out of the room of a loved one who is dying. I was told his orders were always carried out, and no one thought to disobey. It was said that Walter Davidson was in charge right up to the end.

By 1944, Arthur Davidson was the only founder left to guide the sons on how to run their fathers' business. Founder William A. Davidson died in 1937, Walter Davidson in 1942, and William Harley in 1943. Arthur told the next generation of Harleys and Davidsons, "Don't hesitate to call me if you need advice. I will help you in whatever way I can."

Arthur missed his brothers and his friend Bill Harley, but he was proud of the way all their sons got along and were learning the family business. He knew the day would come when he would join the other founders, and only the children would be left to run the company.

My grandmother continued all the traditions that my grandfather had set up and soon was known as the matriarch of the Davidson family. She continued to have lavish parties and travel all over the world—the more exotic the country, the better—only now she invited her women friends to accompany her.

She was a classy lady who expected respect when we were in her presence. I was even taught to curtsey and was expected to do so when we arrived at her house.

My grandmother, like my late grandfather, was always looking for something new to do. Because she was wealthy, she could buy or do whatever she desired. In 1945, she saw an old farmhouse in Menomonee Falls. She soon discovered that it was one of the finest examples of pre-Civil War architecture still surviving in Wisconsin. That was all she needed to hear. She bought it, and her new quest in life was to restore it to its original style. Her goal was to buy only primitive pieces of furniture that would have been in a home of this time period.

On Fridays, she had her chauffeur drive her and her lady friends out to the farmhouse where they would have ice cream and play cards. On some Sundays, my family was invited to the farmhouse. It was like stepping back in time to another period.

The farmhouse was a showplace and not a home to be lived in, however. I was not allowed to touch anything. I thought to myself, "What a dumb house!" All these rooms with lots of neat things and nothing could be played with. It didn't matter much to me in the end, though, because I was always out in the barn practicing my own form of tightrope walking on the high roof beams in the hayloft.

Arthur Davidson At the Races, 1949

Chapter 15

The Birth of a Boy Brings Joy—and Sadness—to Our Family

With the death of my grandfather Walter at the beginning of 1942, my father and mother were saddened, but they knew he had left a wonderful legacy to follow. They always dreamed of having one more child and hoped it would be a boy to carry on the family name. Their prayers were answered, for on December 7, 1942, my little brother was born. They named him Gordon Scott Davidson, and called him Scotty. Gordon, after my father, and Scott, in remembrance of Margaret Scott, my father's grandmother who had married Alexander Davidson and journeyed to America.

These years for my family were filled with joy and family togetherness. My dad did not want to travel. He remembered how much he had missed his parents when he was young, so he chose to only go on trips where he could take us along. Besides, my dad's life was the company, and he would not miss work for any reason. He worked six days a week.

Life now seemed complete. My father was vice president of

Scotty, 1943
My little brother Scotty's first birthday. I am on the left and my sister Barbara is on the right.

the company. He and my mother had three children, one of them a son to carry on the family name.

But on February 7, 1946, our family was struck by tragedy. Scotty, who was then three years old, was accidentally killed in a terrible household accident. He was going to surprise my mom by washing up before his nap and somehow touched the faucet handle and the plug to the heater at the same time. It was a frightful accident, and my mother felt it was her fault for not preventing it.

When I walked home from school that day with my friends Jill Levis and Judy Boettcher, I saw all these cars parked in front of the house and thought it was strange that my mom did not tell me she was having a party. We went to the back door to go in and play, but my Uncle Bobby stopped us at the door and told my friends to go home. I was angry because he didn't say it nicely, and I couldn't understand why they could not stay to play.

Being only eight years old, I didn't believe my little brother could be gone forever. I argued with everyone that he was coming back soon, and they should stop being so sad. At the funeral, I was very naughty and argued with everyone that my little brother would be coming home soon. Obviously I did not understand what dying meant, and everyone was too sad to try to explain. Maybe they tried and I would not listen.

My mother spent most of her days in her bedroom with all the shades down. I remember standing at the door wanting to go in and talk to her but being afraid to upset her. The atmosphere in our home was one of total sadness. I felt completely alone in the world.

Fifty years later, my mother wrote in her memoirs that she could not think or do anything for herself during that time because the pain was unbearable. She just wanted to be left alone to suffer in anguish.

His name was never mentioned again in our family. At the

bottom of the front staircase was a picture of this beautiful blond three-year-old boy, and next to the picture was always a fresh red rose every day. My home had changed from one of lightness and laughter to darkness and sadness.

I was already a strong-willed child who loved the outdoors, so now I turned to the outdoors for all my comfort. I felt no one was able to talk to me at home and I was so lonely. I would sit on the hillside behind my home and have long conversations with God. I talked out loud, telling Him my dreams and thoughts and whatever schemes I was thinking of at the time. I loved roaming around at night, sneaking out when everyone else was asleep. Looking up at the nighttime sky, I believed that the stars were my family and the moon was my light. I guess I never felt I was naughty because God knew everything I was up to, and being my best friend, He approved.

I was often naughty before, but now I really became rebellious. I'm sure that today psychologists would say that I was crying out for attention. My mother tried to help me, but it was hard enough for her to cope with living, much less trying to deal with a child who seemed to always be getting into trouble.

Barbara, my older sister, took the other route. She became even nicer and was good all the time.

My mother wanted to be able to go on with her life, but things were changed forever. She was in such mourning that she and my father decided maybe if they had another child it would help heal the pain of losing their son. It wasn't long before she was pregnant again. The new child was due in February 1947, and my mom started to plan for this new arrival. She was afraid of having another child, but she vowed to herself that this time she would never let the baby out of her sight.

My mother did learn to cope with life, yet there was always a sadness that no one would or could talk about. But soon a new baby was due to join our family. My mother anxiously looked forward to that day with a mixture of joy and fear.

On February 19, 1947, the baby arrived and was a beautiful little girl. She was named Christine Clare and became the center of my mother's life. Olga Hagen, a nurse who was a family friend, was hired to help my mother care for this newborn little girl.

Throughout the spring and summer of 1947, my mother was a case of nerves around the baby. She was so afraid she might do something wrong or that my little sister might die like Scotty did that my dad decided it would be good to go on a family vacation. Olga agreed to stay with Christine while my dad, mom, sister, and I left by train for a six-week trip out west and into Canada.

We followed the route my Dad had taken on his motorcycle trip in 1929 with his brother and cousin. When my dad walked into the Harley-Davidson dealerships, many of the dealers remembered him from 1929 when he was the young, seventeen-year-old adventurer. Now he was back with a wife and two children. The dealers loved to see how he had grown up and was now a family man.

We took the train all the way to San Francisco, where we stayed with Dudley Perkins on his ranch. Dudley had opened his dealership in 1914, and it was one of the oldest Harley-Davidson shops. In my eyes, he was my favorite dealer of the whole trip because he had a white horse and let me ride it—the things that make a child happy! At night, we sat around his ranch while he told stories of the fun times he had shared when my dad motorcycled out west to his dealership.

All too soon, the trip was over, and we had to return to reality.

I remember my mother trying to be happy on this trip but it was so hard for her. Her heart was back with her new baby, but she was so nervous when she was actually with Christine that she didn't think she was being a good mother.

Chapter 16

The Original Harley-Davidson Rebel

Once we were back home, everyone tried to make life go on in somewhat the same fashion as before Scotty's death, but my mother was so afraid something would happen to this new baby that she dedicated her life to protecting her. Because my dad was working all the time, she thought it would help her if another adult came and lived with us. She found a wonderful schoolteacher named Rose Kucirek from Necedah, Wisconsin, who taught typing and shorthand at West Milwaukee High School. Rose came to live with us in the fall of 1947. She became a trusted friend for my mother and would stay in the house whenever my mother went out.

I still couldn't understand what was happening. How had this family gone from being so close knit and happy to sad and separated? Today they would call it dysfunctional, but in those days there were no fancy names.

I was still a free spirit who had loved running around outdoors before the tragedy, so it didn't take much imagination to decide that I was going to be the boy in the family now. Maybe I thought I was taking Scotty's place. I just knew I was never going to be a girl. Girls didn't run and jump and climb trees and love the dirty, loud motorcycle races like I did. I even cut my

Independent from the Start, 1940
A portrait of me at age three.

hair like a boy and told people my name was David. One time a bus driver came right out and asked me, "Are you a boy?" I was thrilled by the question; this man actually believed I was a boy.

All my attention focused on becoming a boy and doing everything a boy would do. I bought boy's clothes and even a pair of boy's shoes so I could kick the football farther. I remember my disappointment when I tried to pee standing up and was unsuccessful. I spent most of my days playing football, baseball, and wrestling the neighborhood boys. I was so good at baseball that the Cub Scout team wanted me to play, hoping no one would find out I was a girl. It was a great life. In the winter, I was always skiing, sledding, or ice skating. I ran around in a gang of boys, and we got in trouble all the time.

My poor mother, who had difficulty coping with me before, now really had her hands full. When I would go inside our home for meals or bedtime, I would always feel this unspoken sad-

Growing Up Harley-Davidson, 1940

Going for a ride in the sidecar with my dad when I was three years old.

ness. Luckily for me, no one sent me to any medical or psychological specialist. They were in such mourning themselves that they just let me be and do whatever I pleased. And that was fine by me.

At our lake home, I swam, water skied, sailed, and played at a nearby mink ranch. I ran barefoot and refused to wear a shirt. No matter what any one said, I was not going to grow up into one of those silly, prissy girls who sat around reading books and giggling. Forget curtseying!

At my twelfth birthday party—to which, of course, I only invited boys—one of the fathers asked my mother, "Don't you think Jean should start wearing a shirt?" My mother just looked at him and shook her head in exasperation. She tried to make me wear a full set of clothes, but I would just take off my shirt when I was out of her sight. Why would anyone want to be a girl? They didn't have any fun.

This tomboy phase of my life continued until I discovered that kissing these same boys who were my buddies was great fun. From playing football with them to kissing them was quite a step. I decided some things about being a girl weren't so bad.

My parents built a home on the old Pabst Farm, which was now called the Washington Highlands in Wauwatosa. As children we could walk or ride the bus everywhere. Our household help consisted of Rose, who lived with us and sometimes cooked and watched after Christine; Mrs. Pouch, the cleaning lady; Mrs. Miller, the sewing lady; Mae, the laundry lady; and Bill and Earl, the two gardeners. Of course Bill and Earl were my favorites because I was always outside with them. My mother did not even have to go to the grocery store. I remember every week the phone rang. I would run to it thinking it would be one of my friends, but no, it would be a lady's high voice saying, "Herman's," a home delivery meat market service. My mother

Bathing Beauties, 1942
My dad with Barbara and I (right) at Pewaukee Lake when I was almost five.

would get on the phone and place her order, and they would send a delivery truck to bring our groceries. How many people had a fresh fruit and vegetable man come in his truck each week? I loved to see Nick stop his big open truck in front of the house and bring boxes in with one of everything to choose from. What a treat to pick out fresh vegetables and fruits right there in the house. Added to all these services, we had the milkman, the ice cream man, the cleaners, and the Jaeger Bakery service that came to the door. Did I think everyone had these services? Yes I guess I did.

Wow! That must have been my mother's main household job—just organizing the help. Of course my mom never wanted anyone to have to take the bus home, so as soon as I was old enough to drive, I would take these different people down to their homes at the end of the day.

Every child should have two homes and two sets of friends: winter friends and summer friends. Summers started with the closing of school. We piled in the car and made the trip to our cottage. It was only twenty-five miles from Milwaukee, but we were not allowed to go back to town during the summer. My father would ride his motorcycle back and forth to work. In the beginning weeks of summer, I would miss my school friends, but after a short time, I made new friends. I was not allowed to go to summer camp so I would sail, swim, and run around getting in trouble. It was a wonderful escape from the normal routine of winter. It seemed like a whole new world.

Of course my basic personality did not change, and soon I had ducks and other pets. Every summer, I would get a baby duck from the farm up the road and raise it. It would sleep in our kitchen at night and would follow me everywhere I went during the day. If I went swimming, along came Mickey the duck.

July 4th was a time for fireworks. My dad loved to put on the best fireworks show on the lake. It all started early in the morning with my dad lighting a firecracker off right under my window. That was the signal for a day of fun to begin.

The big show was at night. Stella and all the relatives would come to the lake for the day. We lined up chairs down near the lakeshore as my dad set up his fireworks out on the pier. Boats filled with people came and waited out in the water for the show to begin. It was a grand display. My mother would always be nervous that one of the children would get too close or the noise would wake up the babies. And she was usually right: The noise would scare some of the children, and one of us usually got burned from the sparklers.

I inherited my love of firecrackers from my dad. I always had a pack of firecrackers in my drawer to play with when I got bored. I placed them in dead fish and watched them explode. My favorite prank was to stuff as many as I could under an old tin can to see how high it would soar when the fuse burned

Carrying on the Tradition, 1943
Barbara and I in the same Scottish kilts that my dad and his brother were photographed wearing in 1917.

down and the firecrackers exploded.

My Dad had a glorious antique wood Chris-Craft runabout named *Nodrog* that was his pride and joy. On Sundays he took out the boat and parked it at the end of our pier. He roared the engine and laughed as we raced out to jump in the boat. He never waited long, so if I did not hurry, he roared off to make a few circles and then come back to pick up late comers. Of course, I always thought he was not coming back and that I had missed the boat ride.

Our weekends revolved around the sailboat races, and as soon as I was old enough, my sister and I sailed a Cub boat. We always finished at the back of the pack because she was the skipper and I would not do what she said. One time, we tipped over because I refused to follow her orders. I have been told that they could hear us arguing on the shore.

One time in grade school, I was in the local hardware store where they were selling little painted turtles. Of course, it was up to me to rescue all of them. I thought I was so smart as I stuffed them into my pockets when no one was looking. As I was leaving the store, the irate store owner stopped me. When he found out I was that young Davidson girl, he called my mother and took me home. I remember him sitting in our living room talking with my mom. Both were trying to figure out why I always felt this need to save animals.

My next idea was to save all the animals at the Humane Society, and I drew up plans for my great scheme. It was my dream to make an underground hiding place where I could keep all the dogs and cats, so I started digging a pit in the neighboring field. There they would be safe and never need to be put to sleep. I planned to go to my hiding place after school and feed and love them every day, and they would not bark because they knew they were saved. Somehow I would feed them and take them out for exercise without the neighbors telling my parents.

In my child's mind, I could not fail. I dug and dug, and pretty soon I had a large, wonderful pit. What I didn't count on was rain, however. One day I went out to work on my pit and found it full of water, so I had to wait a couple days until it dried out. By this time, though, my mother discovered my scheme and that was the end of that.

Another great plan of mine was to start a zoo in our basement. One fall, I collected young fish and turtles, and kept them in the laundry tubs in the basement, turning our laundry room into a Marineland. Every day, I would go down and change the water. I remember the laundry lady, Mae, shaking her head because I was always using the tubs. I had pens everywhere, but of course, many of the chameleons and lizards would escape. One time, Rose found a chameleon in her bed. I thought she was going to quit the next morning, but my mom calmed her down. She was not happy with me for a long time afterwards.

I was always saving animals that I thought needed my help. One of my favorite places to go was the bait store where I bought all the frogs and then released them in Pewaukee Lake. When I was a little older, I picked up every free kitten I saw, and then I searched for a good home for it. It didn't take too long before people would see me coming and say, "Oh no, what does she have now!"

I had a particular fondness for reptiles—and especially alligators, perhaps due to the two surprise alligators we had to give away to the zoo. My dad gave me a baby alligator from Florida, and I made a large pen for it in our yard at Pewaukee Lake. Other children came from all over to see this strange new pet. But he got pretty big, and I began wondering what to do with him. He was also not very friendly, and I had to feed him raw meat on the end of a stick. One of the neighbor boys eventually got angry at me for not letting him touch my alligator, so he let him out, and the alligator escaped into the lake. For a long time after that, we were afraid to go swimming in Pewaukee Lake and warned others to watch out for the alligator. People told me he could not survive Wisconsin winters, but I never believed them. I was sure he was out there just waiting for one of us children to come skinny-dipping some night.

Another time, I came home with a skunk. That was the final straw for Mom. She screamed, which terrified my new skunk, and he jumped out of my arms. My mother chased me around the house with a broom while I chased the skunk. Finally, I caught him—and Mom caught me. She laid down the law after that: "Enough is enough. I have let you raise every imaginable pet, but a skunk is not going to live in our house." I was disappointed because the friend that had given me the skunk said he was descented and would make a great pet. I never found out, though, because my mother made me give him back.

Like many children, I dreamed of having a ranch somewhere in the Wild West where I could run away to and live the rest of my life free from interfering adults. My scheme only required one thing: money. My father did not give me an allowance so I had to think of another route to riches. I thought I had the answer. At night, I would sneak into my parents' room and scoop up the change that Dad took out of his pants pocket when he went to bed. I never stopped to think that he might wonder where his change was disappearing to each night. Dreaming of the fun I was going to have on my ranch, I sat on my bed counting my growing stash. I had about thirty-five dollars when one night my dad stormed into my bedroom and asked, "Where is all this money coming from?" He already knew, but he wanted me to admit to stealing it. I was so upset that I got caught: How would I buy my ranch without money?

I cooked up a new scheme and talked my friend Jill into it. My parents were going to have a big party at their house. My plan was to dress up like Indians, storm into the party, and rob them. First, we had to disguise ourselves so no one would know who we were, and once again I came up with the perfect plan.

Birth of Sister Christine, 1947
Barb holds our new little sister, Christine, while I hold our cat, Jinx.

We collected all of my mother's tubes of lipstick and smeared the red lipstick all over our faces and the top halves of our bodies. Then we tied scarves over the bottom halves of our faces. No one would recognize us now!

On the fateful night, we charged into the party—but that's just as far as we got. The guests burst into laughter, but my mother was furious. She dragged both of us into the bathroom and stuck us in the tub, shaking her finger at me yet again and saying, "I do not want to see either one of you until all the lipstick is off your bodies. Then you can come out and apologize to our guests for being so foolish."

In my eyes, it was another brilliant scheme that didn't work out quite the way I planned. The ranch out west would have to wait.

My father showed his affection by wrestling with me. He rough-housed until I hollered with delight. My mother always told him to stop, but I loved it. He would threaten to give me the famous whisker burn, which meant he would rub his rough day-old whiskers on my check. I don't remember him actually ever doing it, but the threat was enough to make me squirm and squeal.

My mother had a hard time showing her affection for me. I craved being hugged, so she did the next best thing. She let me have pets—as many pets as I desired: dogs, cats, rabbits, birds, chameleons, ducks, hamsters, fish, and gerbils. Whatever I wanted, that is, except a horse. So of course I was jealous of anyone who had a horse. Needless to say, I was very spoiled. I would hold whatever pet I had at the time and feel misunderstood and unloved. I was a trying child.

Now that I have experienced motherhood and raised five children myself, I can't imagine how a mother recovers after the death of one of her children. I used to think if it happened to me I would just curl up and die. I am sure that is how my mother felt, but she had my sister and I and a new baby to care for. My father devoted himself to work to ease the pain, but my mother had to cope with everyday family life.

After having a trying child myself, I now understand why she could not cope with me. When you are so sad and on edge yourself, you would not have the energy to try to understand the child in the family that was the naughtiest. The more she couldn't cope with me, the more I acted out.

Was I crying out for attention? Was negative attention better than no attention? Or was I such a free spirit with determination to do whatever I wanted that it would not have mattered what my parents did?

Obeying rules was never one of my strong suits. I didn't like being told what to do—and I was always looking for exciting new things to do.

One winter at my grandparent's house, I went down the front hill to Lake Michigan and ventured out onto the ice. I was having a grand old time, when all of a sudden I heard a huge boom. The ice cracked between where I was and the shore. I was frightened because no one knew I had left the house and was down on the lake where I had been told not to go.

I remember thinking, "How long before someone will miss me?" Would they ever think to come down to the lake and look on the ice? I also wondered, "How long will it take for the ice chunk to drift way out into the lake?"

It was getting dark, and I decided the only thing to do was to jump across the open water to the other side of the ice near the shore. I did and returned to my grandparent's home. I never did tell my parents about my icy adventure.

My grandmother's sister was a character. I loved her because she was rough and tough. My grandmother and her sister Clara were the daughters of a bar owner. When my grandmother married my grandfather, she acquired the role of being a lady. But Clara was another story. She was not sophisticated and didn't want to be.

Clara used to tell me all about her days as a security guard at Schusters Department Store on 3rd Street and North Avenue, where it was her job to catch shoplifters. I would not have wanted to be caught by her. She could swear like a trouper and had a wolf whistle that could be heard a mile away.

Clara never had any children, but she had a loving heart. She and her husband, Joe, lived next door to us at the lake. Always feeling misunderstood and in need of loving, I would spend a lot of time at her house pouring out my heart to her. She would listen and I would go away feeling better.

My parents had charge accounts at most of the finer stores in Milwaukee. The store owners knew I was a young Davidson, so when I walked in, I was greeted by friendly salesladies who tried to sell me anything and everything. They always told me whatever I tried on was made just for me and remarked on how beautiful I looked. It was a great sales racket, and I fell for it hook, line, and sinker. They would say, "Just take it home, Sweetie, and we'll charge it to your parents." I would walk out of the store with bags of clothing, some of which looked terrible on me. Upon arriving home, I would realize how foolish I had been.

One time a shoe salesman didn't have the size I needed, so he talked me into taking a size smaller, saying, "Your feet will shrink."

I was so gullible. It never dawned on me I was a walking charge account with unlimited funds.

I walked home from school every afternoon with my friends Jill and Judy. We stopped at Meyer's drugstore on the corner. Mr. Meyer was always friendly and would ask us what we wanted. We would get ice cream cones or root beer frappees. I would pick out some new comic books, and then as we were leaving I would say, "Charge it!"

On Saturdays, my friends and I took the bus downtown to the Milwaukee Athletic Club, a private club with a swimming pool. We would swim in the morning and eat lunch in their fancy dining room, where we would steal all the breadsticks out of the breadbasket. When we were done eating, I would just say, "Charge it!" Then we would run around the club and try to sneak up to the floor where the men supposedly swam naked. We were never successful.

Growing up without ever thinking about how much something cost gave me a sense of freedom to explore whatever sounded exciting. And to me almost everything sounded exciting. I took lessons in everything, from piano to singing, ballet to tap dancing, elocution to accordion, violin to guitar, acting to singing, swimming to sailing, baton-twirling to ballroom dancing, tennis to golf, horseback riding to painting, snow skiing to water skiing.

As I mentioned, I did not receive an allowance so I never learned how to budget my money. The two most common words in my vocabulary whenever I wanted something were "Charge it!" This was fine as long as I was in a community where everyone knew my parents, but it didn't work so well in other areas. I learned a hard lesson when Grandmother Davidson gave me an all-expense-paid trip to Europe for six weeks. My parents gave me $500 for spending money. I thought, Wow! This is a lot of money! Well, you guessed it: within the first two weeks, I became lonely for home and wanted to fly back instead of taking the famous ship, the *Queen Mary*. I traded in my boat ticket and most of my cash for a plane ticket, and was left with $50 to last for the next three weeks in Europe. I made it, but I sure did not enjoy the feeling of being broke. My family was unhappy that I did not even bring home a gift for my grandmother who had sent me.

Saying "Charge it!" sounds like fun—and it was—but in reality it would have been nice to know how far a ten-dollar bill would go.

I knew that I was different from my friends, but not in a privileged way. In fact, most of the time I was jealous of them. I remember watching my friends and their parents do the dishes and thinking to myself, "Wow, that looks like fun." If one of my friends told me she couldn't go out because she had to do housework, I would ask, "Can I come over and help?" When a friend complained about having to share her bedroom with siblings, I would be envious and dream about how nice it would be to share a room with my sister.

It's always more fun to do something that we do not have to do. Because I never had to do housework at my house, it looked like fun to do somewhere else. When my friends went to summer camp, I wanted to go with them, but my dad said, "I bought a lake home so you could enjoy the summers, and I will not send you to camp."

As noted earlier, my father's brother Walter and his family lived on a country estate in River Hills, Wisconsin. It was a beautiful piece of property next to the Milwaukee River on Milwaukee's north side. His friends and neighbors were people with substantial wealth who chose to live in similar circumstances.

I would go there to visit and felt like I was stepping into a dream world. It seemed they had everything I ever wanted. There were animals everywhere and lots of land on which to run and play. They even had a private dog trainer who raised and trained Labrador retriever hunting dogs.

Uncle Walter and his friends built a private horse stable so their children could have horses, learn to ride, and participate in private horse shows. He rode polo ponies and would invite me to come to the polo matches at Uihlein Field on the outskirts of Milwaukee where his team competed against other polo teams from around the country. At one of those private horse shows, they let me hand out the ribbons to the winners. It was fun, but I wanted to be riding the horses.

My cousins went to private schools, and everything they did sounded more exciting. Even my uncle's friends were exciting. One time I was at their house and Joy Adamson, about whom the movie *Born Free* was written, was there. I sat spellbound listening to the stories of the lions in Africa.

When I would leave my uncle's estate and go back to my home, I would think, "How dull our lives are over on this side of town." If I wanted to go riding, I had to take a bus out to a public stable named Joy Farm, pay $1.25, and ride around in a circle. I did not get to gallop because there would always be some new person in the group who had never ridden, so the rest of us would also have to walk our horses. I was sent to the public school because my father didn't want his children to think they were special.

Now I look back and am thankful for my parents and the way I lived. But at the time, I was sure it was all wrong: wrong parents, wrong place to live. Yes, I thought the grass was definitely greener over at Uncle Walter's house.

Chapter 17

My Love Affair with Motorcycles

I first rode a Harley-Davidson when I was three, but that doesn't quite count as I rode in the seat of a sidecar while my dad drove. I wasn't much older when my dad placed me behind him on the seat of his Harley-Davidson and said, "Hang on!" as we took off. My earliest memories are of the roar of a Harley-Davidson V-twin motorcycle engine.

When I was twelve years old in 1949, Dad came home to the lake on a large Harley 74. It was a big, beautiful motorcycle, and I begged him to let me try riding it. He laughed and said, "No," because my feet barely touched the ground when I straddled it.

That didn't stop me. I kept pestering him, and finally he said, "OK, but don't cry if you get hurt." My mother heard this and naturally did not like the idea at all. In my mind, that made it even more exciting.

Dad showed me which hand controlled the gas and where the brake was. I got on and thought, "This is easy." I turned the throttle all the way open, and at what felt like full speed, I rode that beautiful new Harley right into the lake. Mom screamed while Dad laughed and said, "I told you so."

I burned my leg on the exhaust, but worst of all, my pride was hurt. I immediately made a vow that I would try this venture again as soon as I was a little older.

Me at Speed, 1952

An illustration by artist Paul Smith of me riding my dad's Hydra-Glide from our Pewaukee Lake summer home to Milwaukee to visit a boyfriend. I rode the thirty miles in nothing but a swimming suit and tennis shoes.

When I was fifteen years old in 1952, I wanted to go to Milwaukee to visit a boyfriend. I did not have a driver's license, so I decided to ride the twenty-five miles on a new Harley-Davidson Hydra-Glide that my father had left at the lake. I had been practicing in the front yard since my fateful ride into the lake, so I was full of confidence that I would do just fine on the roads. My only concern was that if I tipped over I knew I was not strong enough to pick up the bike.

It was a grand ride. I was wearing a swimming suit and tennis shoes. I enjoyed the look from other motorists as I zoomed by; I presumed they were not used to seeing a young girl on a motorcycle and was all the more proud for it. When I rolled in the driveway of the boyfriend's house, I gunned the engine to let him know I had arrived. I will never forget the look of shock on his mother's face when she looked out to see this skinny girl in a swimming suit sitting on a big Harley in her driveway and smiling to beat the band.

She came running out and queried me, "What were you thinking? You don't weigh more than ninety pounds! What were you planning to do if the police caught you or you tipped over that big motorcycle?"

I was so proud of my accomplishment that I couldn't understand why she thought it was a foolish thing to do. As usual, I had no answers; I just thought it would be fun and so went right ahead and did it.

Most of my life was spent doing whatever sounded like fun. Water-skiing by moonlight sounded exciting, so a group of us kids pushed my father's Chris-Craft out onto the lake as quietly as we could and then started the engine. What fun we had, whipping around on the lake and taking turns driving and skiing. The big concern was if one of us would fall down, the boat would not be able to find us in the dark of the night. But of course that just added to the excitement.

After I discovered that kissing boys was a fine thing, my interest in boys changed. Yet in my teens, when a boy asked me out on a date, many times the first question out of his mouth was, "Can you get me a motorcycle?" I was often hurt because I wanted him to be only interested in me. Anyway, what did he think? I could just call up my dad and he would give him a motorcycle? No matter how silly it sounded, it happened over and over again.

My answer to this dilemma was to not tell people my last name; I even went so far as saying my name was Smith. I wanted to be sure these boys liked me for who I was and not for what they thought I might get them.

One time, I became good friends with a young man from the other side of town. We shared many good times, and finally I decided it would not make any difference in our relationship if I took him home and he saw how my family lived. He saw the big motorcycle in the garage and the house with all the servants, and our relationship ended because he felt out of place.

Later in life, I heard my future mother-in-law telling her friends her son was marrying a Davidson. She wasn't saying that her son was marrying a wonderful girl, which maybe she thought, but the most important thing to her was that I was a Davidson.

Still to this day I do not openly tell people, " I am a Davidson from Harley-Davidson." I want people to like and accept me for my own unique qualities.

Chapter 18

The Demise of Indian Motorcycles

From almost the beginning of all this motorcycle business, there was a friendship between Harley-Davidson and the Indian Motocycle Company. People talk about the war between Indian and Harley, but the real war was fought out on the racetrack. Behind the scenes, the founders at Harley and Indian were friends. This may come as a surprise to motorcycling folk, but it's true—and there's an entertaining story behind it.

Harley-Davidson founder Arthur Davidson delighted in raising on his Waukesha County farm one of the finest herds of Guernsey cows in Wisconsin. George Hendee, one of the founders of the Indian "motocycle," also raised prize Guernseys. Because of their bovine hobbies and in spite of their motorcycle "day jobs," Arthur and George became close friends and spent hours comparing their cattle businesses—as well as their motorcycle businesses.

On the racetrack, it was another matter. My grandfather used to tell the story of two brothers named Ray and Irv Tursky. Ray was a Harley-Davidson dealer in Madison, Wisconsin. Irv was an Indian dealer in Fond du Lac, Wisconsin. They were great friends when they weren't racing, and one would send the other brother a customer if he could not convince him to buy the motorcycle he was selling. But Ray and Irv, when they were both racing in the 1930s and 1940s, were arch-enemies, going all out for the win. They not only raced the half-mile and mile dirttracks but also the TT races and hillclimbs, and each brother had his own entourage of supporters hooting and hollering for him to win. Each was loyal to the brand of motorcycle he was riding, and it was a well-known fact that once they were on the track, they were there to prove whose motorcycle was faster. But once the race was over, it was back to being family and helping each other out with sales.

Arthur Davidson stood staunchly against racing, as his many vehement editorials in *The Harley-Davidson Dealer* attest. His friend George Hendee was a former bicycle racer, so he naturally aimed his Indians onto the racetrack in search of publicity. When Arthur and George got together, their conversations naturally drifted from cows to motorcycles to many spirited arguments about the pros and cons of racing—all in a gentlemanly fashion, of course.

Throughout the years, the Indian company's financial stability went up and down like a roller coaster. Its successful motorcycles of the 1900s and 1910s put the firm on a strong foundation. But after founders George Hendee and Oscar Hedstrom retired in 1913 and 1915 respectively, the company's new managers jeopardized the firm with unwise investments and stockmarket shenanigans.

In 1930, the once-proud Indian marque was purchased by E. Paul duPont, scion of the wealthy Delaware family whose name was on the grill of DuPont automobiles. Under the new management, Indian revived, but in 1945, duPont sold his control to an investment group led by Ralph Rogers.

Rogers strove to recast Indian as a maker of lightweight motorcycles in a European style. His plan quickly backfired, and in 1950, Rogers resigned and Englishman John Brockhouse took over the Indian name. Brockhouse started using Indian

Indian Versus Harley-Davidson, 1935

The Tursky brothers battle it out, Irv taking the inside on his Indian with Ray to the outside on his Harley. (JHO Collection)

dealerships not to sell the famous Indian motorcycles but as distributors to sell imported English machines that were less expensive because of the devalued English pound. The Indian dealers were not impressed by these new machines, and many were unhappy. Under Brockhouse's management, the last of the great Indian Chiefs rolled off the assembly line in 1953.

When Indian was struggling to stay alive during the Great Depression, Arthur Davidson talked with his brothers Walter and William to find out if there was anything Harley-Davidson could do to help Indian out of its woes. Harley-Davidson had no desire to see Indian forced out of the market. Arthur had not seen his friend George Hendee in a long time, so in 1935, off he went to visit George in New York City. On his way to Springfield, Arthur stopped to pick up his son Arthur H. at Dartmouth.

Arthur H. wasn't allowed to come into the meeting at Indian headquarters, but his father, obviously saddened by the event, told him some of what went on. Having retired in 1915, George, now on the sidelines at Indian, was only a figurehead and rarely consulted on day-to-day affairs. He wasn't quite himself, and his health was failing; when Arthur realized this, he did not talk business. They talked instead about the glorious old days when Indians and Harleys were both icons in their own right. They laughed about how they would sit for hours comparing notes on motorcycles and Guernsey cows. Arthur realized there was nothing he could do to help and returned to his brothers with the sad news.

The 1935 trip to offer a helping hand to Indian ended with Arthur Davidson and Arthur H. returning with empty hands. Arthur H. went back to school and his father returned to work. Not being part of Harley-Davidson management, Arthur H. did not know what specific assistance the Milwaukee firm might have offered its Springfield competitor. They may have considered joint dealerships during the Depression years, or sharing

Fiftieth Anniversary, 1953

By the time the cake was cut to celebrate Harley-Davidson's fiftieth anniversary, the sons were running the firm. From left: William H., Walter C., Gordon, and Bill J. Harley.

Harley And Indian Riders, 1934

The Harley-Davidson and Indian faithful rarely rode side by side, but this team of mixed makes—a Harley at left joined by two Indians—competed together in an endurance run in Minnesota.

development costs on a new motorcycle model or engine. Were they going to offer a loan? Were they thinking of a merger? The true details may never be known.

The demise of Indian in 1953 was seen as a sad affair at Harley-Davidson. I remember my father coming home from work and remarking how he really wished Indian had stayed in business. You would think the management at Harley-Davidson would be cheering, but it was just the opposite. They all knew it was the end of a chapter in American motorcycling history, and there was a lot of talk on why they felt it happened.

Everyone had his own opinion. The famous Indian Chief and Scout were good, solid machines, but some said that the engineering designs were getting long in the tooth and had not been updated with overhead valves as Harley-Davidson had done with its 61 Knucklehead. And while the British motorcycles from Triumph, BSA, Norton, Velocette, Vincent, and other firms were threatening Indian sales, they weren't enough at this point to kill the Indian company.

Finally, after much discussion, my father and the other Harley-Davidson managers felt that Indian's downfall was due to its haphazard support of its dealership network: Indian simply did not have as strong and active a dealer association as Harley. Because of all the changes in management and directions Indian had taken, the dealers lost faith in who was in charge at the time. Arthur never wavered in his belief that for a company to make money, the dealers had to be given special attention and make money themselves. Arthur considered the dealers to be part of the family and always was ready to put them first. When Indian dealers were asked to sell English motorcycles it was too much. They lost confidence in the firm, and the once-mighty Indian Motocycle Company collapsed.

Harley-Davidson wanted to see Indian stay alive. There was Arthur and George Hendee's personal friendship that stretched back to the beginnings of American motorcycling. George

Fiftieth Anniversary, 1953

On September 3, 1953, the founders' sons posed for this official portrait. From left: John Harley, product engineer; Walter C., secretary; William H., president; Gordon, vice president; and William J. Harley, treasurer and chief engineer.

Hendee died in 1943 at the age of seventy-seven, and Arthur died in 1950, but all the founders' sons remembered the long-lasting friendship between Indian and Harley-Davidson, and that friendship remained part of Harley-Davidson's legacy. There was also a belief at Harley-Davidson that it was better to have a competitor in this country who was a friend than to not know where your competition was coming from and what they were up to. There's an old Scottish saying that fit Harley-Davidson's philosophy: "Better the *divil* you know than the *divil* you don't." In hindsight—considering the looming invasion of the European and Japanese motorcycle imports—it was wise thinking.

When Indian was in its death throes at the dawn of the 1950s, Harley-Davidson's board of directors met to consider purchasing its longtime arch-rival. My dad's new generation of management must have talked long and hard about this possibility, weighing the advantages of buying out Indian. The founders' sons met to discuss how they might help Indian to stay alive, or if Harley-Davidson could buy out Indian itself.

Harley-Davidson's and Indian's lines of motorcycles were designed to go head to head with each other on the salesroom floor and on the racetrack. For the everyday rider, it was a choice between Harley's 61 and 74 big twins and Indian's Scout and Chief; for the racer on the starting grid, it was Milwaukee's WR lined up against Springfield's Sport Scout and special big-base Scout. If Harley-Davidson purchased its competitor, the motorcycles would overlap and duplicate each other, offering no advantage.

The additional factory space might prove a boon in the years to come, but for the time being it was too large, too expensive, and too far away.

In the end, Harley-Davidson decided against trying to buy

Indian. Money was tight at the time, and no offer was made for the ailing rival.

And there was one more point to consider, a deep fear that Indian's demise had raised: The knowledge that the grand company of Indian was now history brought many thoughts of "Could this happen to us next? Are we vulnerable?" Harley-Davidson read the writing on wall: If the legendary Indian could fail, Harley-Davidson could be next.

Walter Davidson and Aermacchi, 1970s
To extend the Harley-Davidson line into the lightweight motorcycle field, the company purchased the Italian Aermacchi line at the dawn of the 1960s.

Chapter 19

Elvis Presley, King of the Road

I n the mid 1950s, Elvis Presley was the king of rock and roll, and he had a fondness for Harley-Davidson motorcycles, the two-wheeled kings of the road. As soon as his first records went gold, Elvis bought a Harley, which he rode as if it were a throne.

Elvis waved from the cover of the May 1956 issue of *The Enthusiast*. Inside, an article appeared titled "Who is Elvis Presley?" Of course as a teenage girl, I knew who he was. I remember watching Elvis on TV about that time when my dad came into the room, shook his head, and laughed, "That young man sure can swivel his hips!"

When asked what his favorite motorcycle was, Elvis's answer was a 1956 Harley-Davidson KH. You couldn't ask for a better endorsement than that.

Elvis continued to order the latest and greatest from Harley-Davidson almost annually. And the King never skimped on accessories, either. In 1957, Bob Jameson, who was a dealer in Evanston, Illinois, at the time got a call from Walter Davidson asking him if he had any new Sportsters left.

Bob replied that yes, he had just one.

My uncle Walter then said, "Hang on to that one because this rock-and-roll, hip-swiveling, young singer is coming down your way and wants to buy a Sportster."

The King of the Road
Elvis Presley waves from the cover of The Enthusiast.

Bob told me he waited for Elvis to come but the King didn't show up. Elvis must have found a Sportster closer to home because the next time he was spotted on a Harley-Davidson, it sure enough was a brand-new Sportster.

Chapter 20

Bad Reputation

I n the mid 1950s, motorcycling got a bad reputation. A motorcycle race and the following celebration in the sleepy little town of Hollister, California, on July 4, 1947, changed the public's attitude toward motorcycles forever. Returning to their homes after fighting in World War II, some young men were bored by everyday life, so they bought old motorcycles instead of settling down and headed down the road in search of a new life. Motorcycle clubs like the Hell's Angels, the Outlaws, Satan's Pals, and many others started up, and it was one such gang called the Boozefighters that made newspaper headlines across the country after the Hollister fracas. A good time got carried too far after the Fourth of July races, and soon motorcyclists were drag racing down Hollister's main street, riding bikes into a bar, and terrorizing the town—at least that's the way *Life* magazine and other newspapers told the tale.

Everyone might have forgotten about this one event, but soon the press was also publicizing the doings of the Hell's Angels and the other motorcycle gangs, portraying them as the new Public Enemy Number One.

Then, in 1953, motorcycle gangs made the big time. *The Wild One*, a movie loosely based on the Hollister incident, was released starring Marlon Brando as Johnny Strabler, the leader of the Black Rebels Motorcycle Club. The film began with a warning that was designed to scare the public—and did: "This is a shocking story. It could never take place in most American towns—but it did in this one. It is a public challenge not to let it happen again."

The Wild One

I thought The Wild One *and the bad boy image it created was all pretty neat because I was always breaking the rules myself. I sympathized with Marlon Brando's character: All he wanted was to be understood. Just like me.*

Good Old Days of Motorcycling, 1950s

Harley-Davidson offered a model for all ages in the 1950s. The look on Junior's face here says everything about motorcycling.

Brando didn't ride a Harley—he rode a Triumph Thunderbird—but the movie's true bad guy, Lee Marvin as Chino, did. Suddenly, Harley-Davidsons—and all motorcycles—were viewed by the public as bad, and all motorcyclists were branded as "outsiders."

I was in high school at that time, and I enjoyed watching the change. My cousin Willie G. was riding a motorcycle, and he was as clean cut as they came. Then there were the boys who were rough and tough and wore their black leather jackets and boots to school. They loved that bad-boy look that was all the rage. Naturally, every boy who felt misunderstood went out and bought a black leather jacket and started walking and talking like Marlon Brando. They didn't have bikes but they wanted to look like they did. I dated a couple of them, and all they would ever talk about was the wild side of riding a Harley—and of course they pleaded with me to ask my dad to get them a bike. I used to ask my dad about the bad-boy image but he would just shake his head and say, "Kids will be kids."

Still, I thought it was all pretty neat because I was always breaking the rules myself. I saw *The Wild One* and several of the other motorcycle movies of the time and of course was attracted to the wild side of the rider too. I sympathized with the Marlon Brando character: All he wanted was to be understood, just like me.

Motorcycling's newfound bad reputation was tough on the company, however. It was hard for many of the family to accept because Harley-Davidson had always had a good reputation from its founding, its work for both the World War I and II efforts,

Bronson, 1969
Actor Michael Parks portrayed Bronson in the Harley-Davidson-sponsored television show Then Came Bronson. *The wanderer rode a Sportster, which soon became popular as a "Bronson Sportster" with customizing and a special red paint scheme.*

and with the Shriners and numerous police departments around the country. Harley-Davidsons always led the victory parades after World War II and any other parades that took place in Milwaukee, especially the Fourth of July celebrations. Harley-Davidson motorcycles were viewed as being as American as apple pie. Now suddenly motorcycles had a bad reputation, and this tarnished Harley-Davidson's corporate image as well.

The one who hated this new image the most was Harley-Davidson President William H. Davidson, Willie G.'s father. He was vehemently against anything that would promote the bad boys, and as you might expect, Harley-Davidson's response to *The Wild One* and the Hell's Angels was totally negative. The company did not want in any way to be associated with motorcycle gangs or anything that gave motorcycling its new bad reputation; any hint of any sort of extremist image was completely taboo. Bill Davidson fought tooth and nail for decades to retain Harley-Davidson's clean-cut image.

It was during the years, when Marlon Brando became a superstar in *The Wild One* and *On the Waterfront,* that a major change came to the Harley-Davidson line: In 1952, the new K-model was introduced as a lightweight, sports machine. It was a very modern motorcycle for Harley-Davidson, although its engine was still a bit old fashioned. Taking the place of the old WL 45, the K rode on a low-slung frame with hydraulically dampened front forks and rear suspension. The K was launched by the company primarily to battle the British motorcycles that were invading the U.S. market, such as the Triumph twin that Brando rode. But the look of the K was modeled after the popular sporting style of the British motorcycles and was just what the bad boys liked. As the model was developed further and was rechristened as the famous Sportster, the machine became the ride of choice for many a motorcycle rebel and customizer. Harley-Davidson didn't approve of the bad boy look, but the company still saw a way to capitalize on it—even starting way back in the 1950s.

As a public relations campaign to promote what the company viewed as the positive side of motorcycling, Harley-Davidson sponsored the television show that debuted in 1969 titled *Then Came Bronson*. The series featured Michael Parks as Bronson, who rode his Sportster across the country in a never-ending odyssey. The company sponsored the show by loaning motorcycles and promoting the series in its dealer showrooms. In a 1969 bulletin, Harley-Davidson Sales Promotion Manager Duane Unkefer told dealers that "The BRONSON series is motorcycling drama 100%. Every episode in some way deals with the excitement of cycle riding. Featured in the series will be scrambles, race enduros, hillclimbs, etc., and plenty of footage showing Michael Parks (BRONSON) riding his SPORTSTER. . . . " Harley-Davidson issued *Then Came Bronson* posters to dealers, and another bulletin told dealers how to convert an XLH to match Bronson's ride: fit a XLCH gas tank, add a custom headlight and new front end, bob the front and rear fenders, and paint the cycle "Bronson Red," which became an optional color on 1970 models. Harley-Davidson obviously liked this Bronson: He was a chivalrous knight in a black leather jacket, a good-guy version of Marlon Brando's rebel.

After the sale of Harley-Davidson to American Machine and Foundry (AMF) in 1969, attitudes started to change. Late in 1970, the company showed its dealers a semi-chopper "factory custom" that would first be offered for sale in 1971 as the FX Superglide. Interestingly enough, Bill Davidson's son Willie G. was the designer behind the machine that signaled the revolution.

The Superglide used the frame of the regular FL and a Shovelhead Big Twin engine and transmission, but the front

Happy Policemen, 1950s
Motorcycles might have been getting a bad reputation, but the police still used them to catch the baddies.

end was replaced by the long forks of a Sportster, giving it a "chopped" look straight from the factory. The gas tank was the same double tanks of the FLH, but a modern fiberglass seat and rear fender added to the custom look. Everyone loved the Superglide, and Harley-Davidson wholeheartedly embraced its new image.

Nowadays, the company makes tons of money from the bad boy-image. Times do change.

Chapter 21

Playing the Charade

My father never got to enjoy the later years of life. At age fifty-five, he developed lung cancer. The vibrant, fun-loving, handsome man was dying. He kept going to work right up until he was too weak, because he himself couldn't believe that his life was ending. He played the tough guy with his family, friends, and co-workers, never letting down his guard to show how afraid he was. I was only twenty-five years old at the time and couldn't imagine what it would be like not being around this gentle man with his wonderful sense of humor.

My father had always wanted us children to call him "Gordon." I never did get a chance to ask him why. Why didn't we call him Dad or Father? Many teachers and friends' parents would ask me if he was my stepfather. In those days I didn't know anyone who was divorced, so I didn't understand what that meant. It was not until after he died that I started using the words "Father" or "Dad" when talking about him.

When Dad finally went into the hospital, my family and I stayed with him around the clock. I wanted to say "I love you" and give him hugs and kisses, but tradition and the rest of my family said I should not because it would alarm him. As if he did not already know he was dying.

Those were the days of the Big Charade: No one wanted to talk about death. The family pretended that the dying loved one was going to get better, and the dying person played along. When

Board of Directors, 1967

The first Harley-Davidson board meeting following my father's death earlier in 1967.

I walked into his hospital room, he would act like everything was OK. Dying was never discussed. One time when I was leaving his hospital room, I heard a loud thump. I turned around and went back into the room. There was my dad crying. He had thrown a magazine across the room and hit the wall. But when I walked back in, he pulled himself together and wouldn't talk about why he was crying. It was so hard to keep up the charade. Who was fooling whom?

The doctors told us that the reason his demise was so slow was because his heart was so strong. On March 6, 1967, my dad took his last breath, and we were relieved that his suffering had finally ended. Out in the hallway, my dad's brother Walter was crying and saying it should have been him because of how wild he had been in his life, and not his brother Gordon, who had never rebelled.

Tradition called for an open casket, so of course my mother followed the way things were done in those days. I stood in the receiving line, and like I had at my little brother Scotty's funeral some twenty-one years earlier, told everyone as they came by that this was not my father in the open casket and they shouldn't look at him. I wanted people to remember him as the vibrant, fun-loving guy he was and not this empty shell of a body.

The people who came to Gordon McLay Davidson's funeral were a diverse group if ever there was one: A mix of suits and ties, leathers with studs, motorcycle boots and grease. They came from all walks of life: from the "acceptable," like the motorcycle police, Shriners, and everyday motorcycle riders, to the motorcycle gangs, including friends from the Outlaws and Hell's Angels. It was a real tribute to my dad to see them paying their last respects to a man who never put on any airs that he was better than anyone else.

Many of the shop workers remembered me from when I was that little girl who ran around the shop. They told me stories of how they loved to see me come to the factory with my dad and play on the assembly line.

When it came time for the funeral possession, the motorcycle police led, followed by a legion of Harley-Davidson riders. When we went by the factory, the whistle blew, the flag was at half-mast, and the employees lined the street. My father had given his life to keeping alive his father's dream of making the finest motorcycle in the world.

Chapter 22

A Dealership of Our Own

At the ripe old age of twenty-one, in 1958, I thought getting married would be a great idea. I looked around for the cutest guy, one with looks but also a wild personality. It was all exciting. When I picked out the young man that I thought would be a perfect mate, I chased him and caught him. His name was John Oeflein. Now I was about to get married, but did I know how to cook or wash or clean? Not a clue. Because of the way I was raised, I had no idea what was expected from a newly married young woman.

What a surprise to find out that if you put a red shirt in with the white wash, the result was a load of pink laundry. I learned about washing by making many costly mistakes. Cooking was the same story. One time I put a ham in the oven and did not know to take off the plastic wrap. The result was a lot of smoke, to say the least. And sewing! Well, I must have been one of the first people to just throw socks away instead of darning them. I did, however, learn how to knit and started knitting Norwegian ski sweaters, socks, and caps, and it was great to see everyone wearing what I had knitted them.

Marriage, 1959
I thought getting married would be fun, so, in 1958, at the ripe old age of twenty-one, I began looking for a husband. In 1959, John Howard Oeflein and I celebrated our wedding.

My parents had told me more about motorcycle racing than about the facts of life. Those were the days before sex education in school, and I was completely in the dark. I never dreamed you could get pregnant so easily. So, of course, nine months and two days after the wedding, I had my first child. I loved being a mother and playing with my daughter Lori Jean, so I proceeded to have four more children—Jon Johnston, William McLay, Susan Elizabeth, and Peter John. I found I was really good at loving and understanding them. Could it be because I was still a child at heart myself?

I did have a problem with disciplining, however. Because I had been raised with so much freedom, I couldn't see any reason to discipline my own children. When they did something naughty, I would think back to all the naughty things I did and smile, knowing they were just learning to live in this world. Now, it was my turn to talk to the police when they came to my door.

Of course, my children all grew up on mini-bikes, motorcycles, and snowmobiles. My husband and I tried to live a conventional life in Elm Grove, Wisconsin, but I wanted horses and dogs and all sorts of pets for my children. Plus, I didn't fit the stereotype of the suburban socialite. I still ran barefoot in the summer and played baseball with the children. One time, when we were living in a large, elegant home, the doorbell rang. I went to answer it, and the man asked, "Is your mother in?" I laughed and said, "I am the mother."

It wasn't long before I knew I needed to move out to the country. We already had two horses, two dogs, two cats, and an assortment of fish, turtles, and birds. Everyone in Elm Grove knew if they needed to give their pet away, they could bring it over to me, and I would find a home for it. It did not take long before friends were saying, "No, I will not give a home to one of your extra pets."

I had always dreamed of a life in the country, and now I looked for the perfect farm. I found it outside West Bend, Wisconsin, and we moved in with our five children and all our pets.

The children and I thrived and planned to live there forever.

In 1967, my husband John was flying to a sales meeting for his employer, General Cable Corporation. My Uncle Walter was on the same plane. They shared stories and drinks, and Uncle Walter mentioned that George Knuth, the old-time Harley-Davidson dealer in Milwaukee County, wanted to sell his franchise. He had been in business for more than forty years and thought it was time to retire.

It sounded great to John and I. Always in love with the sound of motorcycles, I thought this was the perfect opportunity to reconnect our lives with the company.

Before we made the decision, however, John bought a Harley-Davidson from Uncle Walter, who told him, "Take a month and ride it to Florida. Stop at all the dealers on the way. If you like it, then see me when you come back, and we'll talk business." John packed the saddlebags and took off on his motorcycle adventure, looking like Marlon Brando in *The Wild One* riding off into the sunset while I stayed behind with four small children. At the end of the month, it just so happened that the annual Daytona races were about to start, so John cycled over and met my cousin Willie G. Davidson and stayed for the races. When he came back, he immediately called Uncle Walter and asked, "Where do I sign?"

We bought the Harley-Davidson franchise for Milwaukee County in 1968 and built a new store at 6713 West Fond du Lac Avenue while retaining the south-side store at 1753 South Muskeego Avenue. We named our company Milwaukee Harley-Davidson Inc. and became the largest dealer in Wisconsin. We sold motorcycles, snowmobiles, wetbikes, minibikes, and all the accessories that an enthusiast could possibly want. Our customers ranged from the Milwaukee Police Department to the motorcycle gangs' finest, from the motorcycle clubs to the everyday person who wanted a motorcycle simply for fun. We sponsored motorcycle racers who often came to our house for

Dancing with My Dad, 1959
*My father and I dance to celebrate
my wedding.*

dinner, just like during my years of growing up with motorcycle racers in our home.

Our stores were full of exciting people. One time, a limousine pulled up, and the chauffeur opened the door to let out the president of the Outlaw motorcycle gang. He was wild, rough, and scary looking, but the young woman with him was absolutely beautiful. This never ceased to amaze me because I saw it many times over: A rough-and-tumble motorcycle rider would come in our store accompanied by a beautiful girl. I decided that wildness attracts certain women.

When a customer bought a new motorcycle, we offered a free riding lesson. We would ask, "Do you know how to ride a motorcycle?" Most of the new owners would gladly take a lesson and come back to tell us how much they appreciated the help. But sometimes, the new owner said, "No, it's easy. Just hand me the key!" We would still offer the free lesson, but if he kept refusing, we would just shrug and watch him get on, start the engine, and roar out of our dealership. Sometimes just a couple minutes later, we would hear a crash and the sirens. Sometimes we would see that rider again, and he would moan that he should have taken a lesson.

Many motorcycle club members came in our store. They had a great camaraderie and rode away together on fabulous adventures. Many a time one of them would tell me, "The ride is the adventure. I'm never in as much of a hurry when I'm riding my motorcycle. There is this feeling of being a part of the outdoors that I don't get when I am inside a car looking out." I could never join them, because I now had five children to watch over. Nonetheless, I never tired of hearing their stories.

My husband, John, often brought different motorcycles home, and many times we would escape for a moonlit ride. What could be more beautiful than riding at night under the stars with a gorgeous moon in the sky. The fresh air and the sound of the bike made me feel I was a part of the night and brought back the wonderful memories of riding behind my dad as a child.

Much of our social life was spent with my cousin Willie G., his wife, Nancy, and their children. Willie G. went to work for Harley-Davidson when his father, President Bill Davidson, asked him to bring his creative design talent to work at the company. Willie G. always told the story that he replied, "Yes, I'll pack up my crayons and be right over."

Like the rest of us grandchildren, Willie G. was raised with Harley-Davidson motorcycles as the center of his family life. In the early years, we lived near each other in Elm Grove. After becoming the Harley-Davidson dealer for Milwaukee County, our lives were connected both at work and socially. Our children were the same ages; our dogs were even sisters. Our daughters rode horses together while our boys grew up alongside each other on minibikes, motorcycles, and snowmobiles. We all loved the outdoors and rented campers, loaded up the motorcycles or snowmobiles, gathered all our children, and headed for the country. I have wonderful memories of sharing our lives together while watching our children grow up. In 1973, we bought our farm in West Bend and the next year purchased a summer cottage in Eagle River. Now we had places for all of us to enjoy both the country and the northwoods.

As our own children grew older and needed jobs, they worked at our dealership on the weekends and during summer vacations. It wasn't always easy working at our dealership, however. Our oldest son, Jon, worked in the Parts Department. One time he was alone in the store and wanted to get some lunch. There was a hamburger place called Captain's nearby. Jon thought, "If I run over and buy a hamburger, our store will be OK because I can see the front door. If anyone comes, I'll notice." There was a problem with this plan: Yes, he could see the front door but not the back one. It seems a shipment of motorcycles was delivered earlier and was stacked outside the back door waiting to be uncrated and wheeled into the store. After Jon got his hamburger he noticed a truck backed up to the door. Sure enough, it was loading the still-crated motorcycles. Young Jon yelled but it was too late. Away the truck drove with two brand-new Harley-Davidsons. Hearing Jon scream for the police, the thieves accelerated down the alleyway, and one motorcycle fell out of the truck, but they still got away with the other one.

Our nephew, Pete Glaeser, worked for us for eight years while he was going through medical school at Marquette University before becoming a doctor in Birmingham, Alabama.

"One of the interesting things that I noted about the dealership was the wide variation in customers," Pete remembered. "The Harley-Davidson image seemed to transcend or obscure racial and socio-economic lines, despite the relatively high cost of the motorcycles. Some of the regular customers that I remember included the Zittlemans, a wonderful couple in their seventies who had a matching pair of Harley-Davidson motorcycles. And then there was Ray Klinger of Hartford, Wisconsin, who traded in his 1940 Model EL Knucklehead for a 1977 Model FXE Superglide. He said that he only trades every thirty-five years, and his old motorcycle still ran like new with 38,000 miles

A Dealership of Our Own, 1970s
Our dealership, Milwaukee Harley-Davidson, built a customized 90cc mini-bike for Ronald McDonald to parade around Milwaukee and promote McDonald's charity events. (JHO Collection)

on it. There was Zeke, a black dude who dressed the part in black leathers with all the trimmings. He had a great sense of humor, and we loved to see him come in and share jokes. Joe Stadler, a talented, bright mechanic, had a way of talking with people that displayed his knowledge of a topic without sounding demeaning. He was a great teacher and showed great patience in explaining parts and replacement methods.

"The most important thing I learned from the people who worked at the dealership and many of the customers was that intelligence, humility, self-respect, knowledge, wisdom, etc., were not traits reserved for those with money or degrees!"

Chapter 23

Evel Knievel, All-American Daredevil

I n 1971, Willie G., Nancy, John, all our children, and I were
invited to be special guests of Evel Knievel when he came to
Chicago to put on his death-defying show for the public.
The company provided Evel with his All-American Motorcycle,
a Harley-Davidson XR-750. Harley-Davidson was sponsoring
Evel to promote—perhaps ironically—a better image for motorcycling.

On the way down there, I told the children that anyone who
would do such crazy stunts as jumping a motorcycle over nineteen cars must not be very smart. When we arrived, we found
our way through the masses of people to his trailer. His body-
guards invited us in. Much to my surprise, Evel was gracious
and friendly. He joked with our children and told us stories
about his life. When it came time for him to go out in front of
thousands of people and jump over nineteen cars, I felt like I

Evel Knievel, 1970s
*From a volatile boyhood to ice hockey star, insurance salesman to motorcycle
daredevil, Evel Knievel embodied the American Dream. He was unique
among heroes: He was a living, breathing Superman, able to leap a lineup of
Mack trucks in a single bound. (Photograph from Evel and Kelly Knievel)*

already knew this man. He definitely did not fit my idea of some dumb guy trying to get attention.

Evel was born Robert Craig Knievel on October 17, 1938, in Butte, Montana. A copper-mining boomtown, Butte was infamous as one of the roughest, toughest cities on earth, and it all rubbed off on this young boy. Caught stealing hubcaps when he was a teenager, a victim swore at him, "You're a little evil, Knievel." Apparently he liked the way that rhymed, and Evel Knievel would later become his daredevil nickname.

Evel had a crossed life. He worked the mines in Butte as well as riding bucking broncos in a rodeo, playing semi-pro ice hockey, racing motorcycles on dirt tracks and off road, selling insurance, and even robbing a bank or two. In the early 1960s, he left Butte in his rearview mirror and moved on to greener pastures. He ran a couple of motorcycle shops first in Butte, then in Spokane and Moses Lake, Washington, where he built his own dirt-track raceway. He needed a gimmick to sell all those shiny new bikes, so he decided to become a motorcycle daredevil on the weekends.

As Evel Knievel, he would jump just about anything on his motorcycle. He leaped over rows of cars, a tank full of sharks, and once, over thirteen Mack trucks. He started off riding Triumphs, then switched to Nortons and American Eagle-badged Laverda motorcycles before being sponsored by Harley-Davidson.

Evel had style. He wore a red, white, and blue jumpsuit that made him look like Elvis Presley on wheels. In the 1960s and early 1970s, he became an all-American hero like no other.

For his show in Chicago, we sat in the front row and watched intently as he warmed up his Harley-Davidson. It was very exciting, and we all crossed our fingers that he didn't get hurt or killed. The crowd yelled and cheered until finally Evel made his final approach. His jump went just as planned, except they had to open the doors at the end of the auditorium because he was going so fast there was not enough room for him to stop.

We were all supposed to go out that night, but Evel did not show up. His wife came and told us, "Before Evel jumps he needs lots of people around him to get him excited, but after he jumps, he collapses and goes to bed."

I found him to be an interesting person. When I talked to him before the show, he seemed perfectly calm and logical—even though he made his living jumping motorcycles.

Chapter 24

The Sale and Buy-Back of Harley-Davidson

I n the mid 1960s, several Harley and Davidson family members wanted to diversify some of their assets. Most of their assets were Harley-Davidson stock that had been given to them by the founders. Two of the largest shareholders were the founders' sisters, Bessie and Janet Davidson. They had been given stock by their brothers in thanks for Bessie's work keeping the books for years and for Janet's contributions to supporting her brothers. Bessie later gave her stock to her only son, Tiger Marx. Janet never married and gave her money to her church, the Boys and Girls Clubs of Milwaukee, and other charities. But it was the family members who were not working at Harley-Davidson who were the ones who wanted to diversify so they could use the money to invest in their own business ventures. They were now concerned, as the old adage went, that all their eggs were in one basket.

Being a privately owned company, family members did not know how much his or her stock was worth. So the board called in the Robert Baird investment firm to evaluate the stock. It was a difficult job because the accountants had nothing to base the stock valuation on or anything to compare it with. Finally, the figure came in: Each share was deemed to be worth twenty dollars.

The board of directors and most family members thought this figure was too low, but the Robert Baird accountants insisted their valuation was reasonable, so that is where it stayed. Once the price was set, the stock could now be sold, so family members who wanted to diversify could. In 1965, Harley-Davidson went public.

It wasn't long after the company went public that another firm attempted a hostile takeover. Bangor Punta Corporation of Vero Beach, Florida, moved in a like a hungry shark to buy up Harley-Davidson shares in 1965 in an effort to take control of the family firm. Bangor Punta was involved in everything from railroads to building sailboats to Piper airplanes; the managers thought Harley-Davidson would be the jewel in the corporate crown.

Bangor Punta was aggressive. The firm sent agents to knock on the front doors of Harley and Davidson family members' homes and try to buy stock then and there with cash offers. I talked recently with former Rockford, Illinois, dealer Bob Jameson whose father was the famous "Hap" Jameson; Bob said when he was working at Harley-Davidson through those years, Bangor Punta was approaching anyone and everyone who had any stock and offering them money for it. Naturally, Bangor Punta's hostile attack put Harley-Davidson on a frenzied, panicky defensive.

To fight off Bangor Punta, the Harley-Davidson board of directors went in search of a friendly buyer for the company. Within a few months, the directors believed wholeheartedly that they had found such a potential buyer in the Outboard Marine Corporation (OMC) of Waukegan, Illinois. Founded in 1909, Outboard Marine would later become owner of the outboard-motor builders Volvo-Penta, Johnson, and Evinrude—the later founded of course by Arthur Davidson's old chum Ole—as well as the Cushman motorscooter company.

Harley-Davidson was offered to Outboard Marine at a cost of twenty-three dollars per share, which today would seem a bargain. But much to Harley-Davidson's surprise, Outboard Marine's board declined the purchase. Their reasoning? Outboard Marine did not want its name associated in any way with the bad-boy image and tarnished reputation of motorcycling. It was a tough blow for the Harley-Davidson directors and families.

Harley-Davidson's board then started the search for a buyer once again. In late 1968, the directors recommended selling to American Machine and Foundry (AMF) of Mechanicsville, Virginia, a conglomerate of smaller firms making products from bowling balls to billiard tables and other family entertainment and sports equipment.

I remember going to the stockholder meetings and listening to the arguments for and against the sale. There was a lot of yelling and much sadness. I remember thinking that I was glad that my father did not live to see this; he would have been sick just being a part of the family arguments.

Through this whole process, Harley-Davidson President William H. Davidson thought the family was turning on him. He did not want to sell out the company to anyone. The family members who were not working at Harley-Davidson wanted to liquidate their stock.

I was young and didn't really understand what was going on. I had stock that I had inherited, but my father had died, and I felt so alone without anyone to direct me or inform me on what was happening.

After the final decision was made to sell out to AMF, I remember Uncle Walter walking by me and whispering in my ear, "Sell all your stock—right away!" I just looked at him and thought I would be disloyal to my father's memory if I did that.

The sale took place in January 1969, and as time played out, Harley-Davidson stock became AMF stock. I of course should have listened to my uncle's advice. The stock started going down and down and still further down until it was at an all-time low.

Bill Davidson stayed on as Harley-Davidson president under the control of AMF and its chairman, Rodney C. Gott, who was himself a motorcyclist, having learned to ride on a Harley VL in the early 1930s. In 1971, Bill was made Harley-Davidson chairman, but he really had no power under AMF's control; he was the chairman of a board that never met. At the same time, AMF named John O'Brian and then Gus Davis as president, marking the first time that someone other than a Davidson sat in the company president's chair.

Other Harley and Davidson family members continued on at the company under AMF's rein. Bill Davidson's son John was vice president of sales, moving up to become president after Gus Davis. And of course there was Willie G.

William J. Harley—Bill Davidson and my dad's old friend—was engineering vice president until his death in 1971. His brother John Harley remained at the company until his death in 1976 as the last Harley at Harley-Davidson.

On February 26, 1981, a group of Harley-Davidson executives signed a letter of intent with AMF to purchase the company. On June 16, 1981, the deal was finally completed. Harley-Davidson was again a private company, and Willie G. was one of the owners along with AMF's Vaughn Beals, Harley-Davidson President Charles Thompson, and several others.

By the time of the buy-back I was out of the scene because I no longer had any stock in the company. John and I had divorced, and I was living in the northwoods of Wisconsin at our summer home in Eagle River. My husband kept the Harley-

Davidson dealership for another six years. In 1984, he sold the franchise and started a new life for himself.

I remember hearing that a group of people were trying to buy back the company and that my cousin Willie G. was one of them. Even though he was out of the company, Willie G.'s father, William H., never gave up the dream that Harley-Davidson could be something grand. In his heart, he believed that Harley-Davidson could be what the founding Davidson brothers and their friend William S. Harley started and lived by so many years ago. He backed his son with cash so Willie G. could be one of the new owners to lead Harley-Davidson into the future.

Willie G. has developed his talents to the fullest. I am glad that he is representing the Davidson legacy at Harley-Davidson. He reinforces my strong-held belief: Find your unique gifts, develop them, and then use them to serve yourself and your community. It is a tribute to all that I believe in when someone like Willie G. has stayed with our grandfathers' dream of working to make the Harley-Davidson motorcycle the best it can be.

The Old Shed, 1940s
The first Harley-Davidson "factory" survived for many years in the shadow of the new works.